FODOR'S
MADRID
1987

Editor: Margaret Sinclair
Area Editor: Hilary Bunce
Editorial Contributors: Robert Brown, Harry Eyres, Ailsa Hudson, John Mayor, Tom Szentgyorgyi, Pamela Vandyke Price
Executive Editor: Richard Moore
Cartography: Swanston Graphics
Drawings: Beryl Sanders

FODOR'S TRAVEL PUBLICATIONS, INC.
New York & London

Copyright © 1987 by Fodor's Travel Publications, Inc.

All rights reserved under International and Pan-American Copyright Conventions. Published in the United States by Fodor's Travel Publications, Inc., a subsidiary of Random House, Inc., New York, and simultaneously in Canada by Random House of Canada Limited, Toronto. Distributed by Random House, Inc., New York.

ISBN 0-679-01384-9
ISBN 0-340-40068-4 (Hodder & Stoughton edition)

No part of this book may be reproduced in any form without permission in writing from the publisher.

The following Fodor's guides are currently available; most are also published in a British edition by Hodder & Stoughton.

Country and Area Guides

Australia, New Zealand
 & the South Pacific
Austria
Bahamas
Belgium & Luxembourg
Bermuda
Brazil
Canada
Canada's Maritime
 Provinces
Caribbean
Central America
Eastern Europe
Egypt
Europe
France
Germany
Great Britain
Greece
Holland
Hungary
India, Nepal & Sri Lanka
Ireland
Israel
Italy
Japan
Jordan & the Holy Land
Kenya
Korea
Loire Valley
Mexico
New Zealand
North Africa
People's Republic
 of China
Portugal
Province of Quebec
Scandinavia
Scotland
South America
South Pacific
Southeast Asia
Soviet Union
Spain
Sweden
Switzerland
Turkey
Yugoslavia

City Guides

Amsterdam
Beijing, Guangzhou,
 Shanghai
Boston
Chicago
Dallas & Fort Worth
Florence & Venice
Greater Miami & the
 Gold Coast
Hong Kong
Houston & Galveston
Lisbon
London
Los Angeles
Madrid
Mexico City &
 Acapulco
Munich
New Orleans
New York City
Paris
Philadelphia
Rome
San Diego
San Francisco
Singapore
Stockholm, Copenhagen,
 Oslo, Helsinki &
 Reykjavik
Sydney
Tokyo
Toronto
Vienna
Washington, D.C.

U.S.A. Guides

Alaska
Arizona
Atlantic City & the
 New Jersey Shore
California
Cape Cod
Chesapeake
Colorado
Far West
Florida
Hawaii
I-10: California to Florida
I-55: Chicago to
 New Orleans
I-75: Michigan to Florida
I-80: San Francisco to
 New York
I-95: Maine to Miami
New England
New Mexico
New York State
Pacific North Coast
South
Texas
U.S.A.
Virginia
Williamsburg, Jamestown
 & Yorktown

Budget Travel

American Cities (30)
Britain
Canada
Caribbean
Europe
France
Germany
Hawaii
Italy
Japan
London
Mexico
Spain

Fun Guides

Acapulco
Bahamas
Las Vegas
London
Maui
Montreal
New Orleans
New York City
The Orlando Area
Paris
Puerto Rico
Rio
Riviera
St. Martin/Sint Maarten
San Francisco
Waikiki

Special-Interest Guides

The Bed & Breakfast Guide
Selected Hotels of Europe
Ski Resorts of North
 America
Views to Dine by around
 the World

MANUFACTURED IN THE UNITED STATES OF AMERICA
10 9 8 7 6 5 4 3 2 1

CONTENTS

FOREWORD v

FACTS AT YOUR FINGERTIPS 1
Warning 1; Sources of Information 1; When to Go 1; Climate 1; National Holidays 2; Getting to Madrid 2; Visas 2; Health Certificates 2; Customs on Arrival 3; Time 3; Money 3; Costs in Madrid 3; Credit Cards 5; Tipping 5; Mail 5; Telephones 6; Electricity 6; Closing Times 6; Drinking Water 6; Convenient Conveniences 6; Bullfights 7; Customs 7 .

MADRID—HUB OF A NATION 9
The Prado as Starting Point 11
Map of Madrid 12–13
From the Plaza de España to the Victory Arch 19
Old Madrid 21
Excursions from Madrid 27
Practical Information for Madrid 28
Map of Madrid Metro 29
Hotels 30
Restuarants 34

SPAIN AND THE SPANIARDS 53

SPAIN'S HISTORY AND ART 62
Map of Classical Iberia 63
Map of Medieval Spain 68
Map of Hapsburg Europe 72

WINES OF SPAIN 84
Map of Wine Regions 88

EATING IN SPAIN 94

BULLFIGHTING FOR BEGINNERS 101

ENGLISH-SPANISH VOCABULARY 109

INDEX 117

Map of Spain 120–21

Discover the Europe only the natives know.

Avis features GM cars. Opel Corsa

Get a free "Personally Yours" itinerary when you rent from Avis.

Highlights of Germany. Undiscovered Spain. Irish castles and palaces. And much more.

Personally Yours℠ is a customized itinerary, tailored to your own special interests, featuring detailed driving instructions, hotel and restaurant suggestions...plus out-of-the-way places only the natives know about. Be sure to ask for *Personally Yours* when you reserve in advance.

Avis tries harder to make you feel right at home in Europe. Starting with low SuperValue Rates on a wide variety of cars. And your very own personalized itinerary. No wonder we're Europe's largest car rental company. Call your travel consultant, or Avis at **1-800-331-2112.**

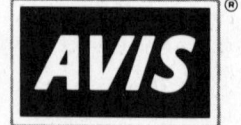

Avis. So easy.℠

Personally Yours is available in selected European countries. Advance request required. Ask for details.
© 1986 Avis Rent A Car System, Inc., Avis®

FOREWORD

Madrid is Spain's focal point in more ways than one. The center for political and social life, it also lies at the country's geographic heart. From it, roads and rail lines radiate out to every part of the peninsula, making excursions nearby or farther afield eminently easy. As an ancient capital, Madrid can offer riches to the visitor in search of historic or, especially, artistic interest. As a city that, in just a few short years, has welcomed the 20th century with open arms, it has a great deal to offer to anyone in search of the joys of modern metropolitan life. Climactically the picture is mixed. The summer, especially August, can be stiflingly hot. Winter, on the other hand, can be pleasant with temperatures rarely below freezing; spring and fall are the best times to go.

We offer this guide, abridged from our *Fodor's Spain 1987*, as a handy book for anyone whose visit to Spain is limited to Madrid and its surroundings. For anyone needing a fuller treatment of the country, then the larger guide is recommended.

All prices quoted in this guide are based on those available to us at the time of writing, mid-1986. Given the volatility of present-day costs—especially unpredictable since Spain's recent entry into the E.E.C.—it is inevitable that changes will have taken place by the time this book becomes available. We trust, therefore, that you will take prices quoted as indicators only, and will double-check to be sure of the latest figures.

Be sure also to double check all opening times of museums and galleries on the spot. We have found that such times are liable to fluctuate with no notice at all, due to staff illness, strikes, fire and Acts of God. You could easily make a trip only to find a locked door.

We would like to stress that the hotel and restaurant listings in this guide represent a selection only of the wealth of establishments available. But errors are bound to creep into any publication. When a hotel closes or a restaurant's chef produces an inferior meal, you may question our recommendation. Let us know, and we will investigate the establishment and the complaint. Your letters will help us to pinpoint trouble spots.

Our adresses are:

in the U.S.A. Fodor's Travel Publications, 201 East 50th Street, New York, NY 10022;

in Great Britain, Fodor's Travel Publications, 9–10 Market Place, London W1N 7AG.

LANGUAGE/30

For the Business or Vacationing International Traveler

In 30 languages! A basic language course on 2 cassettes and a phrase book ... Only $14.95 ea. + shipping

Nothing flatters people more than to hear visitors try to speak their language and LANGUAGE/30, used by thousands of satisfied travelers, gets you speaking the basics quickly and easily. Each LANGUAGE/30 course offers:
- approximately 1½ hours of guided practice in greetings, asking questions and general conversation
- special section on social customs and etiquette

Order yours today. Languages available: YIDDISH (available fall '86)

ARABIC	INDONESIAN	PORTUGUESE
CHINESE	IRISH	VIETNAMESE
DANISH	ITALIAN	RUSSIAN
DUTCH	TURKISH	SERBO-CROATIAN
FINNISH	JAPANESE	SPANISH
FRENCH	KOREAN	SWAHILI
GERMAN	LATIN	SWEDISH
GREEK	NORWEGIAN	TAGALOG
HEBREW	PERSIAN	THAI
HINDI	POLISH	

To order send $14.95 per course + shipping $2.00 1st course, $1 ea. add. course. In Canada $3 1st course, $2.00 ea. add. course. NY and CA residents add state sales tax. Outside USA and Canada $14.95 (U.S.) + air mail shipping: $8 for 1st course, $5 ea. add. course. MasterCard, VISA and Am. Express card users give brand, account number (all digits), expiration date and signature.
SEND TO: FODOR'S, Dept. LC 760, 2 Park Ave., NY 10016-5677, USA.

FACTS AT YOUR FINGERTIPS

WARNING. There has been a huge increase in street crime and in hotel room thefts all over Spain since the early 1980s. You would be well advised to check your valuables into the hotel safe and carry only a minimal amount of cash and one credit card with you. Keep your money in your pocket, not in a handbag or pocketbook. Additionally, women should avoid carrying bags, particularly shoulder bags which are easy to snatch. Make sure your jewelry is not visible, and keep purses as small and unobtrusive as you can. If you have a car, lock everything in the trunk.

Thefts are by no means confined to dark or dangerous streets. Many happen in broad daylight and on crowded main roads. Tour-groups visiting monuments have been set on, and pickpockets are even known to have been at work in the Seville tourist office.

We stress that it is your money and not your personal safety that is at risk. But to make sure that you do not help boost these sorry crime statistics, take extra care at *all* times and your vacation should not be marred.

SOURCES OF INFORMATION. The major source of information for anyone planning a vacation to Spain is the Spanish National Tourist Office.

Their addresses are:

In the U.S.: 665 Fifth Ave., New York, N.Y. 10022 (tel. 212–759–8822); 845 N. Michigan Ave., Chicago, IL 60611 (tel. 312–944–0215); 4800 The Galleria, 5085 Westheimer, Houston, TX 77056 (tel. 713–840–7411); San Vicente Plaza Bldg., 8383 Wilshire Blvd., Suite 960, Beverly Hills, CA 90211 (tel. 213–658–7188); Casa del Hidalgo, Hipolita & St. George Sts., St. Augustine, FL 32084 (tel. 904–829–6460).

In Canada: 60 Bloor St. West #201, Toronto, Ontario M4W 1A1 (tel. 416–961–3131).

In the U.K.: 57 St. James's St., London SW1 (tel. 01–499 0901).

WHEN TO GO. The tourist season runs from the beginning of April to the end of October. If your primary aim is to sightsee, then undoubtedly the best months to visit are May, June and September, when the weather is usually sunny and pleasant without being overbearingly hot. At the height of summer, during July and August, Madrid can be rather unrewarding; not only is it hot and airless but, despite the Tourist Office's efforts to keep the city alive for visitors, you will find many places closed, especially restaurants.

Climate. The whole of the central tableland of Spain, the Castilian plateau with Madrid as its nucleus surrounded by cities such as Avila, Segovia, Toledo, Cuenca and Burgos, suffers (by European if not American standards) extremes of temperature from summer to winter. The keyword to Madrid's climate and to that of much of Spain, is unpredictability.

Average afternoon temperatures in Fahrenheit and centigrade:

Madrid	Jan.	Feb.	Mar.	Apr.	May	June	July	Aug.	Sept.	Oct.	Nov.	Dec.
F°	47	51	57	64	71	80	87	86	77	66	54	48
C°	8	11	14	18	22	27	31	30	25	19	12	9

FACTS AT YOUR FINGERTIPS

NATIONAL HOLIDAYS 1987 The following are national holidays when stores, businesses and many museums and monuments will be closed all over Spain. January 1 (New Year's Day); January 6 (Day of the Three Kings, Epiphany); April 16 (Holy Thursday—some cities only); April 17 (Good Friday); April 19 (Easter Monday—certain cities only); May 1 (Labor Day); June 18 Corpus Christi (second Thursday after Whitsun); July 25 (Santiago); August 15 (Feast of the Assumption); October 12 (El Pilar); November 1 (All Saints); December 8 (Immaculate Conception); December 25 (Christmas Day). In addition to the above, every town and village has its own local fiesta when, with the exception of restaurants, everything will be closed, eg. March 19 (San José) is a holiday throughout the Community of Valencia (Castellón, Valencia and Alicante provinces), and May 2 throughout Madrid province.

GETTING TO MADRID. By Air from the U.S. From North America there are direct flights from New York, Miami and Montreal. Airlines include *Iberia, Spantax Airlines* (Charter) and *T.W.A.* Typical fares as of mid-1986 for New York to Madrid: $1,770 one-way First Class year-round; $1,075 one-way Business Class year-round; $509–$722 roundtrip APEX depending on season.

By Air from the U.K. London is linked with Madrid by the national carriers, *Iberia* and *British Airways,* and there are also prolific charter flights.

By Train from the U.K. To reach Madrid from London it is best to travel via Paris. The distance from Paris to Madrid is some 1,450 km. (900 miles). There is only one daytime train; this leaves Paris Austerlitz at 6.50 A.M. and you arrive in Madrid just before 10 in the evening. There are also two overnight services. The first of these is the *Madrid Talgo,* with sleeping cars, dining car and bar car. It leaves Paris (Gare Austerlitz) at 8 P.M. and arrives in Madrid (Chamartin) at about 9 A.M. the next day. The other is the *Puerta del Sol* which leaves Paris around 6 P.M., reaching Madrid at 10 A.M.; it has couchettes and carries cars, thus forming part of the Motor Rail service.

Advance reservations for these long distance trains are essential, particularly for sleepers and couchettes.

By Bus from the U.K. *Eurolines* operate a service from London Victoria Station to Madrid on four days a week. In Spain the bus calls at San Sebastian, Vitoria and Burgos. The fare is around £120 return full fare, £108 for students. Students must prove eligibility by showing an I.S.I.C. or student union card.

Details of Eurolines services may be obtained from any National Express bus station, appointed travel agent or direct from *International Express,* 237–239 Oxford St., London W.1 (tel. 01–439 9368), or from *Eurolines,* 52 Grosvenor Gardens, London SW1 (tel. 01–730 8235).

By Car from the U.K. Direct to Santander from Plymouth by *Brittany Ferries,* a 24-hour voyage, or to St. Malo—also by Brittany Ferries—or to Le Havre by *Townsend Thoresen* or *P&O.* If making for Madrid, drive down the west side of France to enter at Irun. A night crossing and one hotel night will get you there.

VISAS. Neither American, British nor Canadian citizens need a visa to visit Spain. Americans are allowed a six-month stay after each entry. Britons are allowed a three-month stay instead. Australians and New Zealanders are advised to check current visa requirements before they travel.

HEALTH CERTIFICATES. Not required for entry to Spain.

FACTS AT YOUR FINGERTIPS

 **CUSTOMS ON ARRIVAL.** Each person (aged 15 and over) may bring into Spain 200 cigarettes or 50 cigars or 100 cigarillos or 250 grams of tobacco if arriving from European countries, double quantities if you are arriving from elsewhere. You are also allowed to bring in 1 liter of alcohol over 22° proof, or two liters under 22° proof and two liters of other wines; ¼ liter eau de cologne and 50 grams perfume; gifts to the value of 5,000 ptas. (2,000 ptas. for children under the age of 15).

 **TIME.** During the summer Spain is six hours ahead of Eastern Standard Time, seven hours ahead of Central Time, eight hours ahead of Mountain Time and nine hours ahead of Pacific Time. During the winter, Spain puts her clocks back one hour, but as all America does likewise, the time difference remains the same. Spanish Daylight Saving Time begins at the end of March and ends at the end of October, so during April and October, Spain is seven hours ahead of EST.

Similarly, Spain is one hour ahead of British Summer Time and, during the winter, one hour ahead of Greenwich Mean Time.

 **MONEY.** You can take an unlimited amount of pesetas into Spain, but it's wise to declare any quantity above 100,000 ptas. Any amount of foreign currency can be taken in but you can only take out the equivalent of 300,000 ptas. if on business; for tourists the amount is 120,000 ptas. It is generally better to change traveler's checks in banks than in hotels, restaurants or shops where the rate of exchange may not be quite as good; however, many Spanish banks take an enormous commission charge so there may not be much difference. Always ask the bank what its commission is *before* you change money; if it exceeds 1½% take your business elsewhere.

The unit of currency in Spain is the peseta. There are bills of 500, 1,000, 5,000 and 10,000 ptas.; you may also come across some of the old 100 ptas. bills and although these are being phased out, they are still legal tender. Coins are 1 pta., 2 (rare), 5, 10 (rare), 25, 50 and 100 ptas. At presstime (mid-1986) the exchange rate was around 140 ptas. to the U.S. dollar and 210 ptas. to the pound sterling. However, these rates will change both before and during 1987.

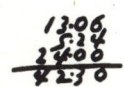 **COSTS IN MADRID.** Prices have soared dramatically over the past decade. Moreover, in January 1986 Spain joined the Common Market which led inevitably to yet another increase in the cost of living. Though at presstime the full impact of Spain's E.E.C. membership remained to be seen, the consequent levying of a sales tax, known as I.V.A., had already begun to cause consternation for Spaniards and visitors alike. I.V.A. has a complicated sliding scale structure, but is usually levied at 6% and this applies to restaurants and most hotels. Luxury, or 5-star, hotels are subject to 12% tax, however, and worse still for the visitor, car rental now falls into the luxury goods category and carries a whopping 33% tax. The days when Spain was the bargain basement of Europe are now over, and the visitor will most probably find that the cost of living in Spain matches that of its northern European neighbors.

Hotels. Spanish hotels have raised their rates in leaps and bounds in the last few years, and since as from 1986 all hotels must now charge the I.V.A. sales tax, they are no longer the bargain they once were. Hotels are officially classified from 5-star to 1-star; hostels and pensions are classified from 3-star to 1-star. If an R appears on the hotel plaque, the hotel is classed a *residencia* and does not offer full dining services; breakfast and cafeteria meals may be available. The star-ratings equate roughly with our classifications of Deluxe (L), Expensive (E), Moderate (M), and Inexpensive (I). The number of stars a hotel has is usually—but not always—a guide to its price. Prices charged by each establishment are listed in the *Guía de Hoteles* (published annually and obtainable from bookstores) and should also be on display at the reception desk.

In many hotels rates change according to season and they are always quoted per room and not per person. Sometimes the rate includes breakfast but often this is charged extra. It is also worth checking to make sure you won't be charged for meals you don't take. If you stay more than two nights you have a right to full board terms, which should be the room price plus not more than 85% of the total cost of breakfast; lunch and dinner charged separately.

It is often advisable to inspect your room before you check in; most hotels offer good standards but it is not unknown for an impressive lobby to camouflage shabby rooms upstairs.

Approximate prices for a double room are shown below. A single person in a double room will be charged 80% of the full price. Many of the larger new hotels have double rooms only. If you ask for an additional bed in your room, this should not cost more than 60% of the single room price or 35% of the double room price. Remember that the I.V.A. tax will be added on to your final bill; in the case of 1-star to 4-star hotels I.V.A. is charged at 6%, and in the case of luxury, or 5-star, hotels at the rate of 12%. Remember that if you are planning to pay your bill by credit card, to check beforehand whether your hotel will accept your particular piece of plastic. Finally, should you have a complaint about your hotel, you can enter this in the hotel's complaint book kept for this purpose, report it to the local Tourist Office, or put it in writing to the Complaints Section of the General Directorate of Tourist Activities whose address is: Dirección General de Política Turística, Sección de Reclamaciones, María de Molina 50, 28006 Madrid.

Approximate prices (double room) excluding I.V.A.:

	ptas.
5-star: Deluxe (L)	13,000–22,000
4-star: Expensive (E)	8,000–12,950
3-star: Moderate (M)	5,000–7,950
2-star: Inexpensive (I)	3,500–4,950

These prices should be taken as indicators only and do not include breakfast. A very few hotels, such as the *Ritz* and *Villa Magna,* fall into a super-deluxe category which rates way above our Deluxe (L) rating.

Restaurants. Prices have increased considerably since Spain joined the Common Market in 1986, and unless you stick to the set menus offered by many budget restaurants, dining out can run away with a large portion of your holiday budget. Finding a light, *á la carte* lunch as you would at home is almost impossible, while bread, whether you eat it or not, and mineral water are always charged for. On the plus side, neither a cover not service charge is ever added onto your check.

Approximate prices per person (excluding drinks):

FACTS AT YOUR FINGERTIPS

a picture of a man or a woman or the words *Senoras* (ladies) or *Caballeros* (men, literally knights!) will tell you which way to head.

BULLFIGHTS. The bullfighting season starts at Easter and continues till early October. The best bullfights usually take place at the biggest fiestas and for times and places see our chapter on bullfighting and the relevant section under *Sports*.

Try to buy your tickets from official ticket booths *(despacho oficial);* many other despachos sell tickets quite legally but if they are not "oficial" they will impose a surcharge of around 20% on the price of a ticket. If a ticket booth displays a sign *no quedan localidades* it means there are no seats left; and if it continues *ni entradas* there is no standing room either. Try another ticket office which may not have sold out yet.

Prices are determined by the proximity of the seat to the ring and by its position in the stand. Ringside seats are known as *barreras* and are naturally the most expensive; the cheapest seats are those known as *gradas* which are high up at the back of the ring. You will also have a choice of *sol* (sun), *sombra* (shade), or *sol y sombra* where you start off with the sun in your eyes but as the fight progresses the sun will dip down behind the edge of the ring. *Sombra* are the most expensive but in high summer are well worth the extra pesetas to avoid sweltering or being blinded by the relentless sun.

Always ask the starting time when you buy your tickets. This varies between 4.30 and 7 P.M. depending on the place and month of the year. Be punctual—there is an old saying that the only things that start on time in Spain are bullfights and Mass—for once the corrida begins, you are not allowed in. Allow plenty of time to find your seat which is not always easy in a large ring. Look closely at the numbers on your ticket, *tendido* is usually the gate through which you will enter the ring, and *fila* the row in which your seat is located. Cushions to sit on can be rented for a small fee and are a must unless you like sitting on hard stone benches with no back support. Most corridas last 2½–3 hours and there is usually a break between the third and fourth bulls which, if you have had enough, is the best time to leave.

CUSTOMS. If you propose to take on your holiday any *foreign-made* articles, such as cameras, binoculars, expensive time-pieces and the like it is wise to put with your travel documents the receipt from the retailer or some other evidence that the item was bought in your home country. If you bought the article on a previous holiday abroad and have already paid duty on it, carry with you the receipt for this. Otherwise, on returning, you may be charged duty (for British residents, VAT as well).

Leaving Spain. Tourists leaving Spain rarely have to go through a customs check, though it is just possible that you will be asked how much Spanish currency you have on you. Officially, you are not allowed to leave Spain with more than 100,000 ptas. in cash.

U.S. Residents. You may bring in $400 worth of foreign merchandise as gifts or for personal use without having to pay duty, provided you have been out of the country more than 48 hours and provided you have not claimed a similar exemption within the previous 30 days. Every member of a family is entitled to the same exemption, regardless of age, and the exemptions can be pooled. For the next $1,000 worth of goods a flat 10% rate is assessed.

FACTS AT YOUR FINGERTIPS

Included in the $400 allowance for travelers over the age of 21 are one liter of alcohol, 100 non-Cuban cigars and 200 cigarettes. Only one bottle of perfume trademarked in the U.S. may be brought in. However, there is no duty on antiques or art over 100 years old. You may not bring home meats, fruits, plants, soil or other agricultural products.

Gifts valued at under $50 may be mailed to friends or relatives at home, but not more than one per day of receipt to any one addressee. These gifts must not include perfumes costing more than $5, tobacco or liquor.

If you are traveling with such foreign-made articles as cameras, watches or binoculars that were purchased at home or on a previous trip, either carry the receipt or register them with U.S. Customs prior to departure.

Canadian residents. In addition to personal effects, and over and above the regular exemption of $300 per year, the following may be brought into Canada duty-free: a maximum of 50 cigars, 200 cigarettes, 2 pounds of tobacco and 40 ounces of liquor, provided these are declared in writing to customs on arrival. Canadian Customs regulations are strictly enforced; you are recommended to check what your allowances are and to make sure you have kept receipts for whatever you may have bought abroad. Small gifts can be mailed and should be marked "Unsolicited gift, (nature of gift), value under $40 in Canadian funds." For other details, ask for a Canadian Customs brochure, *I Declare*.

British residents. There are two levels of duty free allowance for people entering the U.K.; one, for goods bought outside the E.E.C. or for goods bought in a duty free shop within the E.E.C.; two, for goods bought in an E.E.C. country but not in a duty free shop.

In the first category you may import duty free: 200 cigarettes or 100 cigarillos or 50 cigars or 250 grammes of tobacco (*Note.* If you live outside Europe, these allowances are doubled); plus one liter of alcoholic drinks over 22% vol. (38.8% proof) or two liters of alcoholic drinks not over 22% vol. or fortified or sparkling wine; plus two liters of still table wine; plus 50 grammes of perfume; plus nine fluid ounces of toilet water; plus other goods to the value of £28.

In the second category you may import duty free: 300 cigarettes or 150 cigarillos or 75 cigars or 400 grammes of tobacco; plus 1½ liters of alcoholic drinks over 22% vol. (38.8% proof) or three liters of alcoholic drinks not over 22% vol. or fortified or sparkling wine; plus five liters of still table wine; plus 75 grammes of perfume; plus 13 fluid ounces of toilet water; plus other goods to the value of £207 (*Note.* Though it is not classified as an alcoholic drink by E.E.C. countries for Customs' purposes and is thus considered part of the "other goods" allowance, you may not import more than 50 liters of beer).

In addition, no animals or pets of any kind may be brought into the U.K. without a license. The penalties for doing so are severe and are strictly enforced; there are *no* exceptions. Similarly, fresh meats, plants and vegetables, controlled drugs and firearms and ammunition may not be brought into the U.K. There are no restrictions on the import or export of British and foreign currencies.

MADRID

Hub of a Nation

Madrileños, as the citizens of Madrid are called, are fond of claiming that the only better place to be is Heaven. Certainly Madrid is unique, a Mediterranean city nearly 480 km. (300 miles) from the sea, graced most days of the year by a flawless intensely blue sky. Given this piercing light and lack of rain, it is little wonder that Madrid has developed into a city where work tends to be seen as the interlude between bouts of pleasure. Madrid and its inhabitants exude a warmth unique in Spain. The stranger feels irresistibly buoyed up by the vivacity of the people, their friendliness and quick humor. The streets are charged with energy. Madrid is a city that turns foreign visitors into residents.

By European standards Madrid is a relatively recent capital. It was only in 1561 that Philip II decided to fix the court in Madrid, then a small, inconsequential town of some 30,000, mainly very poor, inhabitants. His decision was governed by the fact that Madrid lies at the geographical center of the Iberian peninsula. Today its central position is often compared to the hub of a wheel from which all the main road and railroad lines radiate outwards like spokes to the farthest corners of Iberia.

Yet Madrid remains an odd place for a town, a plateau protruding 600 meters (2,000 feet) up out of the Castilian tableland and the highest capital in Europe. Although Philip II's court had been a byword for austerity, by the second half of the 18th century Madrid was famous among voluptuaries. Casanova came to Madrid for its renowned pre-Lent Carnival and returned to Italy with rapturous reports of its carnal delights. Franco closed down the brothels in 1956 but the enthusiasm with which Madrid has now embraced sexual freedom must cause the old dictator to twirl in his grave.

Madrid city center scores over Berlin, London and Paris by its size. Despite the fact that the city's population has doubled since 1960 and is now around four million, the central area is the same size as 50 years ago. Much of Madrid's charm resides in the fact that it is possible to walk about downtown, with no need to use transport. Turn off any main thoroughfare and you will most likely find yourself in a street of old bars and small artesans, plumbers or carpenters, old-fashioned grocers with shutters fighting the newer supermarkets, with perhaps a Chinese restaurant or a sex shop adding a contemporary flourish. Ambling around the center of Madrid is a pleasure that never cloys.

The rush hours in Madrid are as horrendous as those in any capital of an industrialized country. Madrid lacks the local rail and subway links of Barcelona, so many Madrileños insist on driving to work despite the hold-ups and parking problems involved.

The lack of rain in Madrid means that the city's pollution problem is one of the worst in the world, though of late the government has taken steps to counteract it. It is to be hoped that the newly cleaned-up Manzanares river is only the first in a series of such measures.

Life in Madrid is lived largely on its streets and in its bars and cafes, and there is no better way of sampling the flavor of this most vivacious of cities than by joining in the ritual of twice-daily visits to the city's packed taverns. The morning is interrupted by a coffee break, often a late breakfast. Twelve-thirty is too early for lunch but it is a popular time for the bars to fill with pre-lunch drinkers and those in search of a snack to ward off the pangs of hunger. Restaurants fill up quickly after 1 P.M., their opening time, with those who have only an hour for lunch.

Madrid is not only a Mediterranean city because of the light and the atmosphere but because it also has some of the best seafood in Spain. Every day the pick of the catch is flown to the capital. Some of the most delightful summertime restaurants are a few kilometers out of the city on the roads to Guadalajara, Burgos and La Coruña, where you can eat out of doors: shellfish followed by steak or charcoal-grilled baby-lamb chops, their taste unique in the world.

Instead of sitting down to dinner many Madrileños prefer to go *tasca*-crawling. *Tascas* are small taverns serving tantalizing *tapas*, perhaps black pudding or squid fried in batter, pigs' ears or *mollejas*, bulls' testicles sliced wafer-thin and fried with garlic, a dish for the gods. All bars have tapas, but the tascas concentrate on them and so have a wider range. The tascas are located around the Puerta del Sol, on the Calle de la Victoria and Calle de la Cruz, in Echegaray and on the narrow side streets around the Plaza Santa Ana, home of the *Cervecería Alemana* that Hemingway used to patronize, and on the streets around the Plaza Mayor. In the latter you may chance upon the *tuna*, students

MADRID

playing guitars and clad in the gear of the Inquisition. The tradition is 400 years old and it is worth tipping generously to help keep it alive; as well as their traditional songs they will also play requests.

Madrid's Holy Week processions are not as spectacular as those of more religious cities like Valladolid, Avila or Zamora, but the *Procesión del Silencio* on Good Friday night is nevertheless impressive.

In May the flowers are in bloom and the *económicos* are serving fresh asparagus and strawberries. May 15 is the fiesta of San Isidro, the patron saint of Madrid, an excuse for two weeks of bullfights, fireworks, street festivals and open-air dances. On May 15 it is traditional to drink from the spring at the saint's hermitage just across the Manzanares, where there is an attendant funfair and stalls. This is the authentic San Isidro celebration as portrayed by Goya.

Most Madrileños take their vacation in July or August, and escape to the mountains or the coast. Ten years ago Madrid was deserted in August but gradually as more and more of its citizens have awoken to the charm of scant traffic, cinemas and shops open, and a full program of open-air evening events including opera, operetta, drama and variety performances is organized by the City Council.

Discovering Madrid

To do Madrid ample justice, you need to stay a minimum of three days, after which at least another couple of days or so can be dedicated to excursions to Toledo, Aranjuez, Segovia, Avila, the Escorial and the Valley of the Fallen.

With the exception of the northern reaches of the city around the upper part of the Castellana, Madrid is still a fairly compact capital and you can usually walk from one tourist attraction to another and be assured that enough sights will line your way to reward your efforts. If you get tired, simply take a bus or one of the numerous cabs, still quite cheap, back to your hotel. Or alternatively you can relax in one of the many sidewalk cafes and renew your strength for further sightseeing.

The Prado as Starting Point

Since the attraction most tourists head for first upon arrival in Madrid is the Prado Museum, we will start our tour of the city from this world-famous art gallery, one of the great storehouses not only of Spanish art, but of Flemish and Italian masterpieces.

Located on the main north–south axis, the Castellana (here called the Paseo del Prado), the Prado is best entered through its main entrance on its northern side opposite the Hotel Ritz. Here there is a statue of the artist Francisco Goya. The Prado's other door facing onto the Paseo del Prado, behind a statue of the painter Diego Velázquez, is used mainly as an exit.

The Prado was originally opened in 1823 and has since been superbly stocked with the works of Velázquez, Murillo, Zurbarán, Ribera, Valdés Leal, Alonso Cano, El Greco, Berruguete as well as with a fine collection of Titian, Rubens, Raphael, Botticelli, Correggio, Mantegna

MADRID

0 Miles ¼
0 Kilometers ¼

Points of Interest

1. Archeological Museum
2. Army Museum (Mus. del Ejército)
3. Atheneum
4. Banco de España
5. Casa de Cisneros
6. Casa Lope de Vega
7. Casón del Buen Retiro
8. Cerralbo Museum
9. City Hall (Ayuntamiento)
10. Convent of the Descalzas Reales
11. Lázaro Galdiano Museum
12. National Library
13. Navy Museum
14. Opera House (Teatro Real)
15. Palacio de Liria
16. Parliament (Cortes)
17. Post Office
18. Prado Museum
19. Royal Palace
20. San Fernando Fine Arts Academy
21. San Francisco el Grande
22. San Ginés
23. San José
24. Teatro Español
25. Temple of Dedod
26. Torre de los Lujanes
27. Torre de Madrid; Tourist Office
28. Wax Museum (Mus. de Cera)

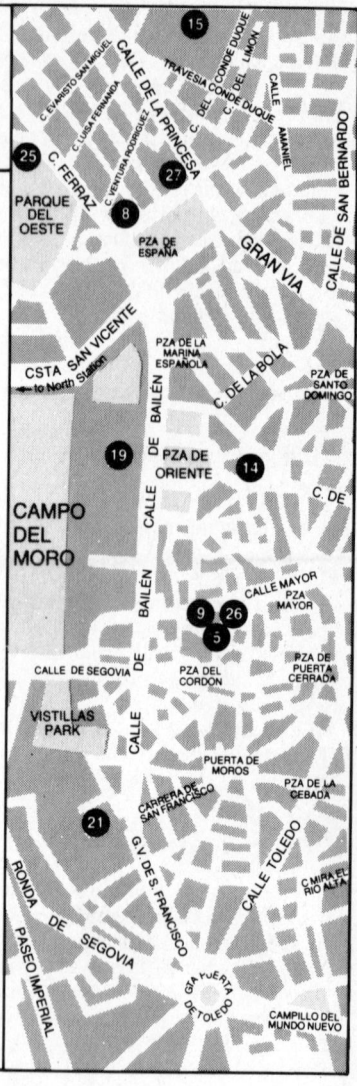

MADRID 13

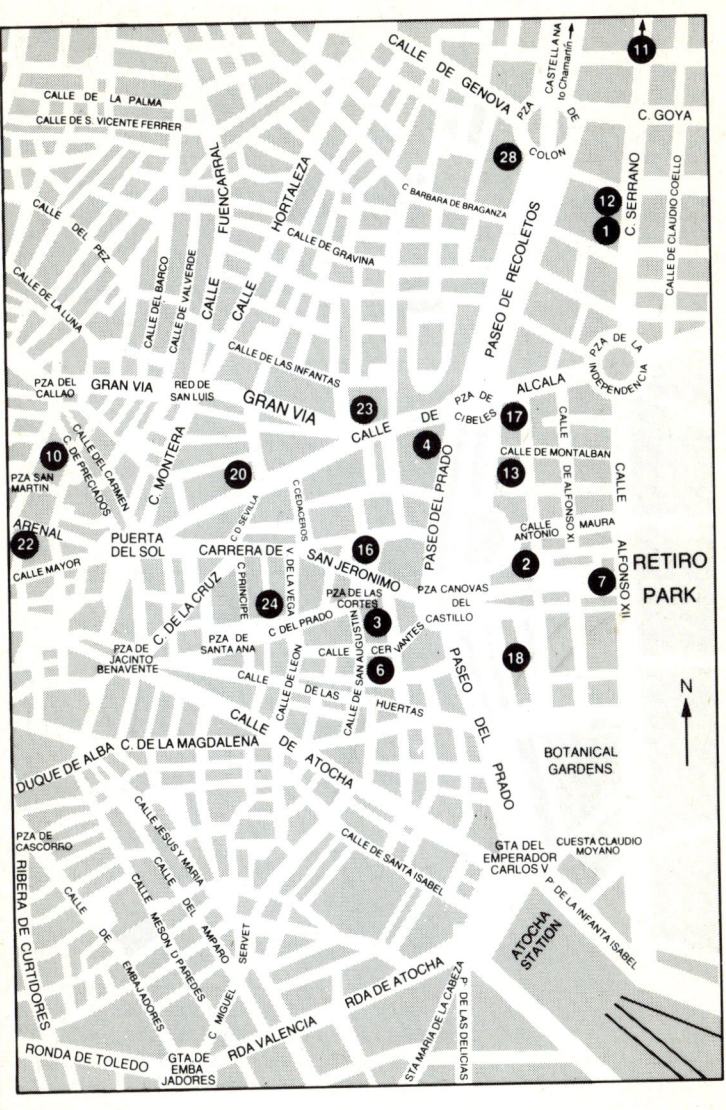

and Bosch which were transferred from the Escorial Monastery outside Madrid where King Philip II had originally housed them. Both he and his father, Emperor Charles V, were avid collectors and brought many art treasures from southern Italy and the Netherlands, both at that time part of the Spanish empire.

To view the Prado's many paintings, statues, tapestries, frescos, numismatic collection and other treasures properly would take weeks. But the highpoints most popular with tourists are usually the El Greco, Goya, Velázquez and Bosch galleries.

The Prado provides a unique opportunity to see the full diversity of Goya's styles. One room is dedicated entirely to the *Caprichos*, well over a hundred of them. Adjacent is a room displaying two of the artist's most famous works, the *2nd of May*, showing the uprising of the Spaniards in 1808 against the French Mamelukes in the Puerta del Sol, and the *3rd of May*, which depicts the execution of patriots by a French firing squad which has the same intensity of reaction to its subject as the later *Guernica* by Picasso. Passing on, you come to a room containing various works from the artist's "black" period, when he was already deaf and living outside the city. The most startling are *The Pilgrimage to San Isidro, Meeting of Witches* and *Saturn*. In another room hang the famous *Naked Maja* and *Clothed Maja*, as well as several portraits of the royal family, including the superb *Family of Carlos IV*, and other earlier works.

One of the most highly regarded Spanish painters over the centuries, Diego Velázquez, also has several rooms set aside for him. In one hangs the *Surrender at Breda*, one of his most impressive paintings. Make sure that you also see *The Drunkards*, and his famous series of four dwarfs. *Las Meninas*, perhaps his most famous work, has been placed in a room by itself, with a strategically placed mirror to help you appreciate its extraordinary complexities.

The main gallery and adjoining rooms contain El Grecos, Riberas, Rubens, Titians and Murillos. You should not leave before visiting the astounding collection of Hieronymus Bosch paintings displayed in the Flemish wing, which includes his famous *Garden of Earthly Delights*, the triptych *The Hay Wagon*, and Pieter Breughel's *Triumph of Death*.

In the fall of 1981 Picasso's *Guernica* was brought to Spain after its years of exile in New York. Its arrival in Madrid was the highlight of that year's celebrations of the centenary of the artist's birth. It is now housed permanently in the Casón del Buen Retiro, an annex to the Prado Museum which stands nearby at the end of the Calle de Felipe IV. The Casón del Buen Retiro is also the home of 19th-century Spanish painting and can be visited on the same ticket as the Prado. On one side of the small square in front of it rises the Royal Academy of the Spanish Language, the learned body charged with safeguarding the Castilian language. It re-edits its monumental dictionary every ten years or so.

In the vicinity of the Prado are three other museums of lesser interest to the tourist on a short stay but nonetheless worthwhile for those with more time to spare. Adjacent to the Post Office on the Calle Montalban is the Navy Museum, small but well-furnished, with ship models, nautical instruments, and Juan de la Cosa's famous map of the New World.

MADRID

At the end of the same street heading towards the Retiro Park is the Decorative Arts Museum, and close to the Cason del Buen Retiro is the Army Museum, fronted by a terrace covered with vintage cannons and mortars. The museum has a good collection of weapons, armor, flags, maps and paintings.

From the Prado to Atocha

After visiting the Prado you could take a stroll through the adjacent Botanical Gardens, opened in 1774 in the reign of Charles III, and come out upon the Cuesta Claudio Moyano, the site of a fascinating secondhand-book market whose stalls offer hours of splendid browsing. A little further on at the corner of Alfonso XII and the Paseo de la Infanta Isabel you come to the Ethnological Museum, of minor interest except to the most dedicated of museum goers. A right turn leads to the Atocha Railroad Station, a colorful 19th-century glass-and-steel structure, which is the terminus for all trains to the south of Spain and to Lisbon in Portugal. The ugly overpass, erected in the Franco years, which straddles the nearby Plaza Atocha, or to give it its full name, the Plaza del Emperador Carlos V, marks the end of the Castellana. The Socialist government has promised to demolish the flyover, an eyesore desecrating what was once an attractive square, and work should begin soon to dismantle it. Quite what will happen to the ensuing traffic chaos remains to be seen. If from here you cross over the southern end of the Paseo del Prado and proceed up the Calle de Atocha, you will enter an old working-class area, well worth a stroll for those seeking offbeat neighborhoods and local color.

From the Retiro to Cibeles

By far the best plan after a bout in the ever-crowded Prado is to take a stroll in the Retiro Park just a couple of streets away. Madrid's prettiest and most popular park, the Retiro dates back to the 15th century, though it was not opened to the public until 1876. Among the park's attractions are a dozen or so outdoor cafes, a lake for rowing, playgrounds for children and shady lanes, often decorated with statues and monuments and fountains, ideal for strolling. In spring and summer, band concerts are held on Sunday mornings, and members of the Catalan colony in Madrid meet and solemnly dance the sardana. The Retiro plays host annually to a dog show, art exhibitions in the 19th-century glass-and-iron Crystal Palace and puppet shows; in summer there is an outdoor movie theater and even outdoor theatrical performances are sometimes staged here.

In addition to the large lake with its huge monument to Alfonso XII, there are two smaller ones, stocked with ducks and swans and surrounded by weeping willows. Fountains, statues and busts, beautiful flower arrangements and a delightful rose garden all help to make the Retiro a welcome haven from the city's bustle. In summer you can enjoy the park till about 10.30 at night.

Leaving the Retiro at its main exit, the Plaza de la Independencia, you'll see a large arch, the Puerta de Alcalá, built in 1778 by Sabatini in Charles III's reign. The arch was formerly one of the gates to the city, with an adjoining customs' station; beside it stood the old bullring, which was later moved to its present location on the Calle de Alcalá at Ventas.

If at the Plaza de la Independencia you turn down the Calle de Alcalá, you will come to the Plaza de Cibeles, named after the Greek goddess Cybele (daughter of Uranus) who stands mounted on a chariot. The fountain has become the unofficial emblem of the city. Cibeles, as the square is known to Madrileños, is the great crossroads of the city, the intersection of the Calle de Alcalá and the Castellana. The cafes in the central promenade on the southern side are perennial favorites and here also a small playground, trees and benches make the area between Cibeles and the Neptune fountain an especially inviting place to rest after sightseeing.

The Salamanca Neighborhood and Beyond

The area northeast of Cibeles, the Salamanca neighborhood, is named after the financier José Salamanca who started building this then-new residential area in the 1870s. The *barrio* or neighborhood is bounded on the south by the Calle de Alcalá and the Calle Goya, the latter a busy shopping street lined with shops and branches of the two leading department stores, the Corte Inglés and Galerías Preciados.

You can now proceed north along either the Castellana or the Calle Serrano, the latter being the most elegant and expensive shopping street in the city. The surrounding streets parallel and perpendicular to Serrano are the domain of elegant shops and boutiques as well.

Going up Serrano from the Plaza de la Independencia (Puerta de Alcalá) you come first on the left to the Archeological Museum, a large, sprawling building with sections dedicated to Greek, Roman, prehistoric and Christian and Moorish cultures. Here you can see a reproduction of the Altamira prehistoric caves in Santander, a worthwhile visit since visits to the caves themselves are limited. Beside the museum once stood the old Mint, which has now been torn down to make room for a huge esplanade decorated with olive trees, sculptures by Vaqueros Turcios, allegorical of the Discovery of America, and the statue of Columbus high up on a pillar, which formerly stood in the center of the Plaza de Colón (Columbus Square). Underneath is the airport bus depot, as well as arcades, shops, and the Villa de Madrid theater, a leading cultural center and experimental theater.

Crossing the Calle Goya, you come on the right to the Celso García department store and then on the left to another branch of the Galerías Preciados department store. After passing many sidewalk cafes and art galleries, as well as the American Embassy and the British ambassadorial residence and dozens of boutiques, you finally reach the Lázaro Galdiano Museum.

Housed in what was formerly the luxurious private villa of José Lázaro Galdiano, writer, journalist and antique collector of the early 20th century, the museum contains a magnificent collection of *objets d'art*, all tastefully displayed, which ranges over clocks, paintings from

Spanish and foreign masters, armor, furniture, tapestries, enamels and jewels—in all a really splendid array which is well worth a visit.

If you have walked as far as the Lázaro Galdiano Museum, you may well opt for a bus or cab ride back down the Castellana to Cibeles. If, on the other hand, you decide to brave the streams of fast-flowing traffic and the accompanying exhaust fumes, there are many sights to reward your efforts on this impressive modern avenue. Few of the noble palaces of old remain, but just every now and again, tucked away between glass and concrete structures, you will catch a glimpse of these splendors of yesteryear. Heading south down the Castellana from the Glorieta de Emilio Castelar, you will come to the overpass linking the Paseo de Eduardo Dato to the Calle Juan Bravo. Underneath this is a pleasant garden adorned with several sculptures forming the outdoor sculpture museum, an agreeable place to sit for a while. The Castellana at this point is lined with the embassies of several countries, Finland, Germany and Belgium among them, before reaching the Plaza de Colón. Here in the northwest corner on your right are two large office buildings, the Torres de Jerez, much criticized for their graceless obtrusiveness and architectural non-style. Curiously enough, they were built from the top downwards, using a narrow central tower as a support. Inside one of them is the famous Chicote's bottle museum with its 10,500 bottles formerly housed in the basement of Chicote's bar on the Gran Vía. Across the street in the Centro Colón office complex is the Museo de Cera, one of Europe's more worthwhile wax museums. On the other side of the square are the Gardens of the Discovery of America and the monument to Columbus which you will have already seen on your walk up the Calle Serrano.

Continuing on down the Paseo de Recoletos, the first building on the left is the impressive National Library which often features exhibits and art shows in its salons. Next, also on the left-hand side, comes the sumptuous Banco Hipotecario, formerly the home of the Marquis of Salamanca. Then on the right comes the famous old Cafe Gijón, full of nostalgic atmosphere for the time when it hosted some of the greatest *tertulias* (political, literary or artistic discussions) of the capital. It is still worth a visit for those in search of shades of a more romantic past, and in summer tables and chairs are set outside on the avenue's sidewalk in front of the cafe.

Arriving back at the Plaza de Cibeles, the building on the northwest corner is the Ministry of the Army, surrounded by lush gardens and guarded by soldiers. It was originally the palace of the Marquis of Linares, built at the turn of the century. Opposite, on the northeast corner, is the Palacio de Buenavista, built for the Duke of Alba in 1769. It was slated to be torn down, like so many other palaces lining the Castellana, but in 1976 a reprieve came from the government which declared it a national monument.

Cibeles to Gran Vía

On the southeast corner of Cibeles rises the huge, cathedral-like Palacio de Communicaciones which the people of Madrid often jokingly refer to as Nuestra Señora de Communicaciones—Our Lady of

Communications. It is, in fact, the Main Post Office, built in 1918, and one of the landmarks of the city.

On the southwest corner of Cibeles is the Banco de España, analogous to the Federal Reserve Bank in the U.S. In the bank's underground vaults are stored the gold reserves of Spain. The building was finished in 1891.

Progressing along the Calle de Alcalá, on the right is the Church of San José, completed in 1742. Just past the church, branch right onto the Gran Vía, Madrid's answer to Broadway, lined with shops, cafes, newsstands and numerous movie theaters. On the left side you will see the elegant Grassy jewelry store, and on the right Loewe, Spain's leading leather store, and then Chicote's bar, a favorite meeting place during pre-war days and much frequented by Hemingway and other writers.

The small traffic circle you come to next is the Red de San Luis. You can here branch left down the Calle Montera which will take you to the Puerta del Sol, or go toward the right up the Calle Hortaleza or the Calle Fuencarral. The latter is lined with inexpensive shoe shops, and ultimately links up with the "boulevards," a network of avenues skirting the center, which start at Colón and end at the Parque del Oeste. On the way notice the impressive Churrigueresque façade sculpted by Pedro de Ribera in 1722 on what was formerly a hospital. Today the building houses the Municipal Museum, and close by are the Romantic Museum and the Theater Museum. Off to the left in the streets around the Plaza Dos de Mayo is the area known as Malasaña, whose narrow streets are packed with music bars very popular at night with the young of Madrid. It is a lively area and one where you may well be offered *chocolate* (hash). Smoking marijuana is not illegal in Spain, though peddling it is. On the Glorieta de Bilbao is the crowded Cafe Comercial, another of the famous cafes of old.

Back at the corner of the Gran Vía and the Calle Valverde, you'll see the Telephone Building (La Telefónica), at one time the highest structure in the city. During the Civil War of 1936–39, when Madrid remained loyal to the Republic, the Telefónica was the main observation point for Republicans surveying the battleground around the university campus and the Casa del Campo Park, where it was piled stories-high with sandbags. Walking on past the movie theaters with their large canopies, you come on the left to the Plaza del Callao. The main building of the Galerías Preciados department store, together with its annex, takes up most of the square. Two pleasant shopping streets, which are closed to traffic and where benches and flowers have been installed, the Calle de Preciados and the Calle del Carmen, both lead down to the Puerta del Sol. At the lower end of Preciados is the original Corte Inglés department store, which now has branches all over Madrid. If instead you branch right, down the Calle Preciados toward the Plaza de Santo Domingo you come to several excellent restaurants.

MADRID

The Plaza de España to the Victory Arch

Continuing down the Gran Vía past Callao, you pass on the right the Sepu budget store as well as numerous cafeterias, movie theaters, airline offices, hotels, travel agencies and shops. Cross the Calle de San Bernardo (which toward the right takes you to the old university building, the Music Conservatory and then links up with the boulevards) and a few streets on you come to the large, spacious Plaza de España, flanked by two highrise towers, the Torre de Madrid, with 37 floors and the highest building in Madrid, and the Torre de España, the second-highest building with 25 floors. On the ground floor of the former is the Tourist Office, which supplies handy maps and other useful information; the latter houses the elegant Hotel Plaza, long a favorite with American visitors.

A large, three-story garage was built under most of the Plaza de España, but the square, as all others where similar facilities were built, was then tastefully redone. Now the Plaza is a delightful place for reading or relaxing, refreshment. Around the fountain, tourists sun themselves and hippies strum guitars. In the middle of the park stands the statue of Don Quixote and Sancho Panza, as well as a monument to the Discovery of America.

From this square, should you proceed straight ahead up the Calle Princesa, you'll first see on the left a conglomerate of shops and restaurants huddling in the large courtyard of an office building, which has become a popular meeting place for young Madrileños.

On the right of the Calle Princesa stands the Palacio de Liria, privately owned by the Duchess of Alba and open to the public by arrangement only. It is one of the few palaces which still belong to an aristocratic family, and is actually lived in by the much-titled Duchess. Work on it began in 1770. After being badly damaged during the Civil War, it was subsequently rebuilt. A pleasant cafe and a mesón-restaurant in the small park in front of the palace make ideal stopping-off places.

Continuing up the street on the left is the Hotel Meliá Madrid. Further up you come first on the right to the Hotel Princesa Plaza, then on the corner of the boulevards another Corte Inglés department store; there are shopping arcades on either side of the street. Beyond, as far as the Triumphal Arch, is an area known as Argüelles, popular with students from the university of Madrid who come here to drink *cañas* (small draft beers) and eat plates of squid. At the top of Princesa on the left is the Airforce Ministry building, a copy of Juan de Herrera's Escorial, and in front the Victory Arch built by Franco in 1956 to commemorate his triumphal entry into Madrid at the end of the Civil War.

The University City and Moncloa

Beyond the Victory Arch lies the University City, an area with several points of interest but too spread-out to visit on foot. However, it can be reached on city bus routes or by a short cab ride, and its main places of interest can be glimpsed from tour buses on excursions to the Escorial.

The University City was begun in 1927 but was mostly destroyed during the Civil War when it was the battleground for the Nationalist troops besieging Madrid. However, it was rebuilt, though generally in undistinguished style, and is today one of Spain's most prestigious universities, with over 100,000 students, many of whom come from Latin America.

Just off to the right of the Avenida de la Victoria is the Museum of the Americas and, further on, on the left, at the beginning of the Avenida Puerta de Hierro, you will come to the Museum of Contemporary Spanish Art. The word "contemporary" may seem to be something of a misnomer, but it is nevertheless a worthwhile museum. Beyond lies the Moncloa Palace, home of Spain's Prime Minister. At the end of this avenue, Madrid's western limit is marked by the Puerta de Hierro, an iron gateway built in 1753 by the Bourbon monarchs who used to come hunting around El Pardo. The road which branches off to the right here leads to the Zarzuela Palace, home of King Juan Carlos, and eventually to Franco's former home, the palace of El Pardo, now a museum.

From the Plaza de España to the Casa de Campo

At the Plaza de España you can take an alternative route. Walk to the other side of the square, cross the Calle Ferraz, and enter the Parque del Oeste (West Park), formerly the Cuartel de la Montaña (a barracks), and you'll come to the Temple of Debod, an authentic Egyptian temple which formerly stood in the Aswan area of the Nile. It was transported stone by stone to Madrid from Egypt when the Aswan area was flooded. The temple and its pleasant surroundings and palm-tree landscaping are well worth a visit.

Crossing over Ferraz, you come to the Cerralbo Museum, formerly the private mansion of the Marquis of Cerralbo. The building is crammed full of paintings, furniture and personal mementos, and is rather less museumlike than the Lázaro Galdiano Museum. Visiting it is akin to paying a call on a nobleman's private quarters at the turn of the century. The mansion was built by the traditional-minded marquis in 1876.

Returning to the Parque del Oeste across the street, you continue up the Paseo de Rosales (named after a 19th-century bohemian painter from Madrid). Lining the paseo are countless outdoor cafes, delightful in fine weather. The park is well cared for. Especially beautiful is a large rose garden, with bowers, a fountain and benches.

At the corner of Rosales and Marqués de Urquijo (the end of the boulevards) is an excellent ice-cream parlor with dozens of exotic flavors. Across, at the corner beside the children's playground, is the end station of the cablecar *(teleférico)* which takes you over the Manzanares river to the Casa de Campo Park, popular with Madrileño families. It is a trip well worth making, for it affords some breathtaking views of the city and the Royal Palace. At either end of the cablecar are restaurants—the one on the Casa de Campo side with outdoor

MADRID

self-service facilities. Buses run regularly from the cablecar station to the zoo and the amusement park. The zoo, in addition to the usual outdoor animals, also features a children's zoo, camel and boat rides, puppet shows, and a good restaurant.

From near the cablecar entrance in the Parque del Oeste, it is possible to make your way down to the Hermitage of San Antonio de la Florida where the church is decorated with Goya frescos revealing the artist's somewhat sarcastic attitude to the Church. Beneath the crypt of the church lies Goya's headless body, brought back to Spain from France in 1888.

Old Madrid

A tour of Old Madrid can best be started from the Plaza Mayor, a few streets down from the Puerta del Sol. This, the oldest section of the city, was built during the rule of the Habsburg dynasty prior to the mid-18th century. Old Madrid is a warren of narrow streets, silent churches and small squares, a welcome respite from the hectic pace and fumes of the city, an area ideal for the cursory wanderer who will let whim dictate his steps and so encounter charming vistas, streets and buildings at each turn. Getting lost here is part of the fun, for you are sure to come out eventually at some imposing monument or church which will act as a landmark.

The Plaza Mayor

The Plaza Mayor measures approximately 110 by 90 meters (360 by 300 feet) in length and width and is one of the most beautiful and also one of the most representative squares in the city. Work on it was begun by Juan Gómez de Mora in 1617 in Philip III's reign and when it was completed in 1620 eight days of merrymaking followed. Fires gutted parts of the structure in 1631, 1672 and 1790; complete restoration was not undertaken till 1853.

In the 17th century the square was used for bullfights and also for *autos da fé* and the burning of heretics, with the king watching from the section called the Panadería (Bakery) in the center of the northern side, while the 476 balconies were full of nobles and dignitaries enjoying the fun. The square was also used for the canonization of San Isidro, San Ignacio de Loyola, San Francisco Xavier, Santa Teresa de Jesús and San Felipe Neri. In it were held masked balls, firework displays and plays, among them those of Lope de Vega.

In 1629 the square was lavishly decorated for 42 days to celebrate the marriage of the Infanta María and the King of Hungary. Here also was celebrated the arrival in 1623 of the Prince of Wales, the future Charles I of England. During his reign, King Philip V turned the square into a market; and in 1810 triumphal arches were raised to receive the Duke of Wellington; later, in 1812 the square's name was changed to the Plaza de la Constitución. And in 1847 the last bullfights were held here to commemorate the marriage of Queen Isabel II.

Until the late '60s the Plaza Mayor was a bustling, commercial square, with buses and trolley cars and traffic noisily clanking through it. But with the crush of tourists invading Madrid, the city decided to close it to traffic. Around 1970 a large parking lot was built under the square, but the cobblestones and the equestrian statue of Philip III by Juan de Bolonia, made in 1616, were dutifully replaced. The cafes could now spread out and strollers relax without being bothered by traffic fumes and noise.

Though the day-to-day vitality of the Plaza Mayor is gone, it is still lined with old shops and taverns; the most famous of the former are the hat and uniform shops where an extraordinary selection of headgear can be bought—anything from a pith helmet to a cabby's tweed cap. Three good restaurants with tables and chairs placed outdoors provide a pleasant opportunity for outdoor lunching or dining. In summer, theatrical performances and the Festivales de España are sometimes held here; before Christmas the square fills with stands selling decorations, noisemakers and Nativity scenes, while all around fir and pine trees are placed on sale. On Sunday mornings the square fills with stamp and coin collectors who cluster on the sidewalks and cobblestones as they buy, sell and swap parts of their collections.

Researching the Mesones

Walking down the time-worn steps under the Arco de Cuchilleros, in the southwest corner of the square, you come to one of the most picturesque tourist areas in the city. The two streets leading from the Calle Mayor down to the Plaza de Puerta Cerrada (marked by a stone cross), the Cava de San Miguel and the Calle Cuchilleros, are lined with taverns and mesones which at night are a-bustle with a merry crowd spearing tapas and drinking beer and wine. To make the taverns still more enticing, many owners hire guitarists and accordion-players to liven things up. Especially on Saturday nights, the area has a touch of carnival about it as tourists and locals spill out onto the streets and the noise reaches a boisterous pitch.

The Cuevas de Luis Candelas, one of the oldest of the mesones, has an old barrel-organ to provide the music. The Cuevas is named after a famous bandit (1806–37) whose exploits passed into the realm of folklore over the years. In an effort to prove its authenticity, the tavern has hired a doorman and dressed him up in a bandit's costume. Some wags feel that it is the tourists instead of the coach travelers who are now being fleeced; but apocryphal or not, the Cuevas is always a fun spot for roving visitors.

From Luis Candelas' you can proceed to the Mesón de Drácula, the Mesón de la Tortilla, or a half-dozen other mesones, each specializing in local foods, which are usually recognizable in their windows where you may see mushrooms frying in oil or omelets being flipped into the air. Most of the taverns are more suited for a drink or a tapa than a full-course Spanish meal. For that, you can go to Botín's on Cuchilleros, one of the quaintest old restaurants in town which makes a determined effort at being picturesque on its three stories crammed with wooden furniture and Castilian knickknacks. The prices are moderate, the rooms oozing with charm, and the crowd of tourists usually impenetrable.

MADRID

Around the corner at the Puerta Cerrada lurks another oldtime haunt, Casa Paco, unbeatable for its thick, juicy steaks served on sizzling plates. This atmospheric and always crowded restaurant began life as a tavern over 50 years ago. If you haven't reserved a table, you will most likely have to wait a while in the bar up front, a not altogether unpleasant fate.

The Royal Palace

Bearing right, the narrow, curvy Calle de San Justo takes you to the Plaza del Cordón and the Casa de Cisneros, originally built in 1515 and restored in 1915. The house once belonged to the son-in-law of Cardinal Gonzalo Ximenez de Cisneros, Primate of Spain and Inquisitor General, much maligned abroad for his role in the Inquisition.

A sharp right takes you up the Calle del Cordón to the Plaza de la Villa, the site of Madrid's City Hall (Ayuntamiento) and the Torre de los Lujanes, where King Charles V supposedly kept his main European rival, François I of France, prisoner for a while after winning the Battle of Pavia. The building is now used by the Hemeroteca Municipal, or Municipal Newspaper Archives.

Continuing down the Calle Mayor, past the Consejo de Estado y Capitanía (Council of State and Captaincy), you come to the Calle de Bailén where, on turning right, you come across the Royal Palace, second only to the Prado as one of Madrid's greatest sights. Beside it stands the stark Cathedral of La Almudena, a modern afterthought which has been ignominiously shrugged off by the Madrileños, who consider it an intrusive pastiche. Construction remains incomplete though work is once again in progress.

The Royal Palace, a magnificent Bourbon structure, stands on the site of the former Alcázar, or fortress, which burned down in 1734. The first stone of the palace was laid in 1737 in Philip V's reign using plans drawn up by Juan Bautista Sachetti, but it wasn't completed until 1764, under Charles III's rule. The palace provided a stylish abode for Spanish monarchs for almost 200 years. Even Napoleon's brother, Joseph, was sumptuously housed in it in the early 19th century. After the French were ousted, King Ferdinand VII moved into the palace. The building remained a royal residence until the coming of the Second Republic in 1931 when King Alfonso XIII left it for exile in Italy.

Though General Franco sometimes used the palace for official state receptions and audiences, he lived in the El Pardo Palace just outside the city, leaving most of the Royal Palace as a museum. King Juan Carlos presently lives in the less ostentatious Zarzuela Palace, also outside the city.

A tour of the Royal Palace takes several hours, and includes visits to the Pharmaceutical Museum, the Royal Armory and the Library. Guides are available at the main entrance and if you really want to appreciate the sumptuous salons with their precious carpets, porcelain, timepieces and chandeliers, you would be well advised to make use of their services. The Coach Museum is at the other end of the gardens and must be entered from that side, a five-block walk away.

Outside the palace is the spacious Plaza de Oriente, enhanced by large stone statues of pre-unification kings and warriors. Originally 108 of them were intended to adorn the roof, but their weight was so great it was considered more prudent to place them in this park and in the Retiro. The Plaza de Oriente has traditionally been used for demonstrations for and against the regimes in power. Across from the palace you can see the Opera House, which after decades of neglect was refurbished and regally opened in 1966 as a concert hall.

San Francisco el Grande

If, on reaching the bottom of the Calle Mayor, you turn left onto the Calle Bailen and walk southward over the viaduct bridge, you pass the pleasant Vistillas Park on the right, and the nearby Plaza de Gabriel Miró commanding some good views, and the studio of the painter Ignacio Zuloaga, before coming to the most important church in Madrid, the basilica of San Francisco el Grande, begun in 1761 by Fray Francisco de las Cabezas and completed in 1784 by Francisco de Sabatini.

The inside decorations date from 1881. Outstanding is the large dome which can be seen from many points in the city. It measures 29 meters (96 feet) in diameter, larger than St. Paul's in London. Paintings in the chapels include works by Goya, Claudio Coello and Lucas Jordán. The 50 splendidly-carved choir stalls originally stood in El Paular Monastery outside Madrid. The fine English organ dates from 1882.

A few streets ahead along a rather bleak section takes you to the Puerta de Toledo, an arch built in 1827 under Ferdinand VII's rule by Antonio Aguado.

Double back up the Calle Bailén and then right to the Carrera de San Francisco, formerly the scene of lively summer verbenas or street festivals during the celebrations in honor of La Paloma, which takes you to the Puerta de Moros square, opposite the Cebada market. The present "barley market" is a relatively new structure and replaced the steel-and-glass one long a landmark of the city. Beyond the Plaza de la Cebada and crossing the Calle de Toledo, go down the Calle de Maldonadas and you come out at the Plaza de Cascorro, the threshold of the Rastro.

The Flea Market

The Rastro, or Flea Market, has long been one of Madrid's main tourist sights, especially on Sunday mornings, but beware, for it is also a haven for pickpockets who fare well among the jostling crowds. It is a sprawling indoor and outdoor emporium that attracts gypsies and art connoisseurs, tourists and dropouts, where you can find anything from a rusty flintlock rifle to a new puppy dog. Despite the fact that decades of bargain-hunters and professional antique dealers have raided the Rastro, new objects turn up constantly, and bargains are still occasionally found if you know what you're after. Some of the wares are wildly overpriced, so watch your step. It really takes repeated visits before you get the hang of it and know which sections to hunt in. Though the most active time is Sunday mornings, the better antique shops are open every day of the week, but not the street stands.

The main thoroughfare of the Rastro is the steep hill of the Ribera de Curtidores, which on Sundays is jammed full with pushcarts, stands and hawkers and gypsies selling trinkets, plastic toys, records, camping equipment, new furniture and foam rubber mattresses. The better wares are usually kept inside the stores on either side of the street.

Those seeking antiques, though hardly at bargain prices, might enter the two sections off the Ribera de Curtidores, about halfway down the length of the street. On the left, the Galerías Piquer is renowned for its choice art pieces, and on the right another Galería is equally reputable. The Galerías each consist of a large courtyard surrounded by a dozen or so antique stores on two levels. To pick through the Galerías carefully takes hours.

Also leading off from the Ribera de Curtidores on the left are two narrow streets, one specializing in the sale of modern paintings and the other selling birds, fish, puppies and other pets.

At the bottom of the Ribera, where the iron junk market starts, you turn right down the Calle Mira el Sol one block and come out on the Campillo del Mundo Nuevo, a square with a park in its center, where among other stands and items spread on tables and blankets, you'll find a book and record fair where bargains can occasionally be found. The Rastro sprawls across the Ronda de Toledo, to the other side of the road, but that section of it is mostly reserved for electrical appliances, old bicycles and spare machinery parts.

Instead walk back up one of the steep narrow streets such as the Calle Carlos Arniches or the Calle Mira el Rio Baja, lined with junk shops and stands, a good bargain-hunting area. Wind up at the Plaza General Vara del Rey, another recommended area surrounded by antique shops and jammed on Sundays with stands of every description.

Vendors start putting away their wares and locking their shops around 2 P.M. at which time you can dip into some tapas at one of the taverns on the Plaza del Cascorro.

Another Stroll from the Prado

Back at the starting point at the Prado Museum, another itinerary takes you across the Paseo del Prado, up past the Palace Hotel to the Carrera de San Jerónimo; on the right stands the Congreso de los Diputados or the Palacio del Congreso, the Spanish Parliament, opened in 1850 and in front of which crouch two lions cast from the molten metal of cannons captured in the war with the Moroccans in 1860. At the back of the Parliament building is the Teatro de la Zarzuela, where Madrid's opera season, as well as many dance recitals, zarzuelas and other shows, are staged.

Crossing the small park in front of the Cortes, and going down the Calle de San Agustín, you come to the Calle Cervantes, on which, at no. 15, stands the house where Spain's famous playwright, Lope de Vega, lived from 1610 until his death in 1635. Close by, on the corner of Cervantes and the Calle León, stood the house in which Cervantes died in 1616. Turn right on León and walk to the Calle del Prado, where in front of you stands the Atheneum, an influential club and cultural center.

Straight ahead you come to the Plaza de Santa Ana, where you'll see the Teatro Español, the government-subsidized theater where Spanish classics are staged in season. It was damaged by fire a few years ago but has now been refurbished. Across the square is the Simeón department store, and above it the old-world Hotel Victoria, much favored by bullfighters in the days when Hemingway was in Madrid. The wood-paneled Cervecería Alemana on one side of the square used to be a popular rendezvous for literati, and in recent years became for a while a bohemian haunt. Today it is a favorite with tourists.

A short walk down the Calle Príncipe, or the Calle de la Cruz, past Seseña, the store specializing in capes, takes you to the Carrera de San Jerónimo, on the corner of which stands the large Banco Hispano-Americano. Going around the building on the Calle de Sevilla and turning right on the Calle de Alcalá leads you to the San Fernando Fine Arts Academy, which contains several recently renovated galleries with works by Goya, Zurbarán and Murillo.

The Puerta del Sol

A few more steps lead you into the Puerta del Sol (Gate of the Sun), among the major crossroads of Madrid and, indeed, of all of Spain. Kilometer distances in the country are still measured from this zero point. On an island in the center stands the symbol of Madrid, a small statue of a bear and a *madroño* (strawberry tree), reminiscent of the time when Madrid was surrounded by hunting forests. Formerly, the Puerta del Sol was famous for its bustling, all-night cafes and hectic traffic. Around it on the Calle de Alcalá and the Calle Arenal a generation of artists and intellectuals thrashed out the problems and theories of an as-yet non-industrial Spain in endless *tertulias* and talk-sessions. Unfortunately none of the cafes remain, and much of the action has moved on to other parts of town. However, the square is still a very lively intersection, as can be seen any evening around 8 o'clock, when the citizens of Madrid begin their ritual evening stroll, the *paseo*. On December 31 it fills with people cheering in the New Year as they watch the golden ball on top of the Dirección General de Seguridad building descending at midnight. Most still follow the old custom of trying to swallow one grape at each stroke of the clock. The large ministry building is now police headquarters. On one corner, the old Hotel París overlooking the square still keeps its vigil. On another is the perennially popular La Mallorquina bakery to which Madrileños with a sweet tooth have been flocking for pastries and sweets for decades. The tearoom upstairs commands a good view of the square.

The Puerta del Sol has been the scene of many stirring events and its history is closely linked to that of the country. The most famous incident that occurred here was the uprising in 1808 against the French, depicted in Goya's painting, *El Dos de Mayo*.

Arenal to the Opera and Calle Mayor

Proceeding on the Calle Arenal, you come on the left to the old Teatro Eslava, now one of the city's leading discos, and next to it the Church of San Ginés. Branching to the right off the Calle Arenal, along the Calle San Martin, you come to the Convent of the Descalzas Reales, founded in the 16th century by Princess Joan of Austria, daughter of Charles V and the Queen of Portugal. In 1559, the Franciscan sisters of Santa Clara moved into the building. Since then it has been lived in by many famous scions of royalty and to this day contains cloistered nuns in one part of the convent. Tours through other sections of the building are provided so that tourists can now admire the superb tapestries and assorted paintings by El Greco, Velázquez, Titian and Breughel the Elder that decorate its historical walls.

The building across the refurbished square (again with an underground garage) houses the Montepío, or Government Pawnbrokers Office; on another side of the Plaza de las Descalzas is a Portuguese fado restaurant and an excellent antiquarian bookshop, Luis Bardón.

Leaving the square at another exit, along the Calle de Trujillos, you come out eventually on the Plaza de Santo Domingo. Turn left down the Calle de la Bola at the far side, then right at the third street and you will emerge at the Plaza de la Marina Española, where you'll see a large building which was the Spanish Parliament in 1820. Originally it housed the Colegio de Doña María de Aragón, one of the earliest university-type institutions in Madrid. Under Franco it was the headquarters of the Falangist Movement, and today the building houses the Palace of the Senate.

You can then continue on to the Plaza de España, or down to the Plaza de Oriente facing the Royal Palace and back around the Opera into the Calle Arenal. Finally, you might like to cut up through one of the old narrow streets linking Arenal with the Calle Mayor, the "Main Street" of old Madrid. As you wander down this historic street, lined with old-fashioned shops selling books, curios and religious objects, look out for no. 50 where Lope de Vega was born in 1562, no. 75 the home of the the 17th-century playwright Calderón de la Barca, and no. 53 glorying in the name of *El Palacio de los Quesos* (Cheese Palace), a shop selling cheeses from all over Spain. Leaving the past behind you, this route brings you out once more in the bustling hub of Madrid, the Puerta del Sol.

Excursions from Madrid

Madrid is ideally situated for side trips as there are several towns and cities of outstanding interest lying within easy reach of the capital. Should you decide to keep your hotel base in Madrid, such places as Toledo, Aranjuez, Chinchón and Alcalá de Henares in New Castile, Avila and Segovia in Old Castile, and the nearby Monastery of El Escorial and the Valley of the Fallen in Madrid province, all lie within 100 km. (60 miles) of Madrid and are easily reached on day trips by

MADRID

private car, on public transport or, in the case of the larger cities, on tour buses which make regular excursions from the capital.

PRACTICAL INFORMATION FOR MADRID

GETTING TO TOWN FROM THE AIRPORT. The least expensive way to travel from the airport to the city center is to take the yellow airport bus to the Plaza Colon terminal on the Castellana. The journey takes approximately 15 minutes. These buses leave the national and international termini at Barajas airport about every quarter hour from 6 A.M. to 11 P.M., and the fare, including baggage, is around 150 ptas. The Colon terminal is underground, taxis meet the buses, and it is only a short ride then to most of Madrid's hotels.

Taxi fares into central Madrid are not prohibitive. The average ride will cost what is on the meter (800–1,000 ptas.) plus surcharges (see *Getting Around* below). If your hotel is in northeast Madrid, on the airport side of town, best take a cab straight away; it will cost only a little more than the combined airport bus and cab ride.

TOURIST OFFICES. The *Spanish National Tourist Office* is on the ground floor of the Torre de Madrid on Plaza de España, near the beginning of Calle Princesa. It is open business hours only, and closed Sat. afternoons and Sun. There is another branch in the arrivals hall of the international terminal at Barajas airport.

There is also a tourist information office run by the City Hall on Plaza Mayor.

TELEPHONE CODE. The area code for the city of Madrid and for anywhere within Madrid province is (91). This should only be used when calling from outside Madrid province.

GETTING AROUND. By Metro. The subway is the easiest and quickest way of traveling around Madrid. There are ten lines and over 100 stations. The metro runs from 6 A.M. to about 1 A.M. Fares are 40 ptas., whatever distance you travel. Subway maps are available from ticket offices, hotel receptions, and the tourist offices at Barajas airport and on Plaza España. Plans of the metro are displayed in every station but rarely in the trains themselves. Many ticket windows close at 10 P.M., so you will need change for the automatic machines at night; otherwise, buy a *taco* of ten single tickets.

By Bus. City buses are red and run from 5.30 A.M. to between 11 P.M. and 2 A.M., depending on the line. The fare is 45 ptas., or 70 ptas. for a transfer. The yellow microbuses, which are airconditioned, cost 50 ptas. Plans of the route followed are displayed at bus stops, and a map of all city bus routes is available free from the EMT kiosk on Plaza Cibeles. A *bono-bus,* good for ten rides, costs 300 ptas. and can be bought from an EMT (Empresa Municipal de Transportes) kiosk. Books of 20 tickets valid for microbuses are available from the kiosk on Plaza Cibeles, cost approx. 900 ptas.

MADRID

A good way to get acquainted with the city is to ride the *Circular* bus, marked with a red C. Its route passes several monuments and a number of the main streets, and a ride will cost you only one ticket. Another good ride is on bus 27 along Paseo del Prado, Paseo Recoletos and the Castellana.

By Taxi. Taxi meters start at 65 ptas., and the rate is 36 ptas. per kilometer. Supplements are 50 ptas. Sun. and holidays, 50 ptas. between 11 P.M. and 6 A.M., 50 ptas. when leaving bus or railroad stations, 50 ptas. to or from a bullring or soccer stadium on days when there is a fight or match, 75 ptas. to sporting

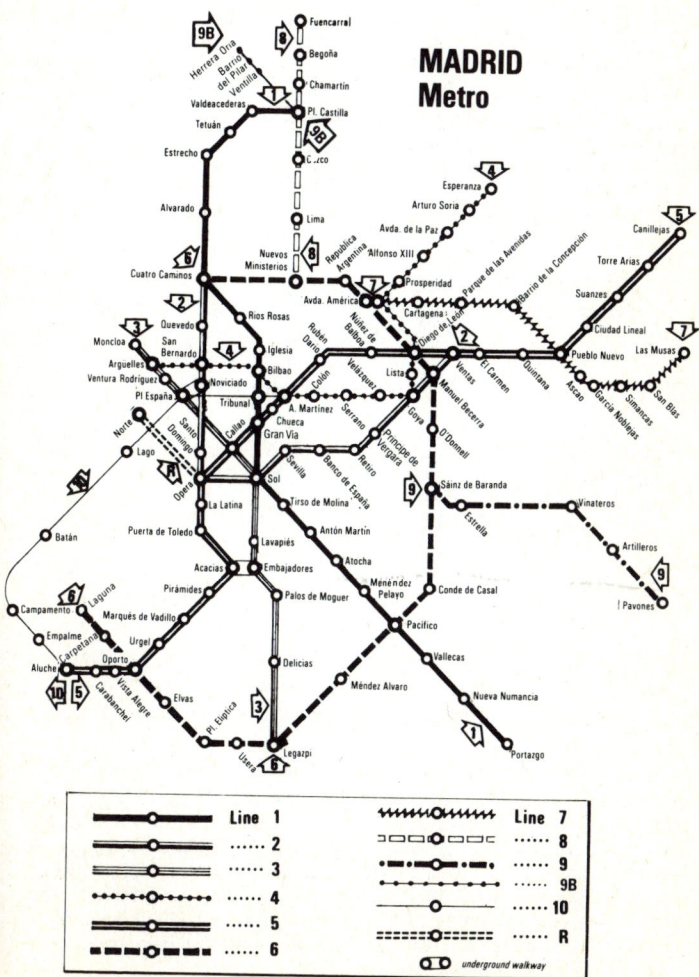

facilities on the edge of Madrid, 150 ptas. to or from the airport, and 25 ptas. per suitcase. Taxis available for hire display a *Libre* sign during the day and a green light at night. Taxi stands are numerous or you can flag them down in the street. Taxis hold three or four passengers. Always check the driver puts his meter on when you start your ride. Tip 10% of the fare. To call a radio cab, call 247 8200/8500/8600.

RAILROAD STATIONS. There are three main stations. Chamartín in the north of the city is the departure point of most trains to the northwest, north and northeast (including Barcelona). Atocha at the far end of Paseo del Prado is the departure point for most trains to Andalusia, Extremadura and Lisbon. Trains to the Levante (Valencia and Alicante) mostly leave from Chamartín, though some depart from Atocha. Always check which station your train leaves from. An underground line connects Atocha with Chamartín. Trains to local destinations such as El Escorial, Avila, Segovia, Guadalajara, and Alcalá de Henares, can be boarded at either station.

The other main station is Estacíon del Norte (North station, or Príncipe Pío), just off Cuesta de San Vicente. There you can get trains to Salamanca, Fuentes de Oñoro, Santiago de Compostela and La Coruña—and all other destinations in Galicia.

For train information and tickets in advance, go to the RENFE office at Alcalá 44, any of the main stations (Norte is the least crowded), or call 733 3000. The RENFE office is open Mon. to Fri. 8–2.30 and 4–7, and Sat. 8–1.30. The advance ticket offices at Chamartín and Atocha stations are open daily 9–9, and at Norte daily 9–7. There is also a RENFE office in the international arrivals hall at Barajas airport, open Mon. to Sat. 8–8, Sun. and fiestas 8–2. Travel agents displaying the blue and yellow RENFE sign also sell rail tickets, at no extra charge, and are a good bet in the crowded summer months.

BUS STATIONS. Madrid has no central bus depot. There are two main bus stations, the Estación del Sur, Canarias 17 (tel. 468 4200), and Auto-Res, Fernández Shaw 1 (tel. 251 6644). Buses to Aranjuez and Toledo, Alicante and many destinations in the south leave from the Estación del Sur; to Cuenca, Valencia, Extremadura and Salamanca from Auto-Res. To other destinations, they leave from all over the city and it is best to enquire at the Tourist Office.

As a guide to some of the more popular destinations, buses to Avila leave from Martín de los Heros 4; to Segovia and La Granja from Paseo de la Florida 11; to El Escorial via Galapagar from Isaac Peral 10, or via Guadarrama from Paseo de Moret 7; to Burgos, Santander and San Sebastián from Alenza 20.

HOTELS. Madrid offers a wide range of hotels, all the way from the millionaire *Villa Magna* to modest little pensions where you can get a room for around 1,500 ptas. a day. For a capital city, Madrid's accommodations are very reasonably priced and standards are mostly high. Many hotels are fully booked at Easter and around July and August. There are hotel accommodations services at Chamartín and Atocha stations, and at both the national and international airport termini. All hotels have all rooms with bath unless stated otherwise. For a guide to prices, see page 18.

MADRID

Super Deluxe

Ritz, Paseo del Prado 5 (tel. 221 2857). 156 rooms. Conservative, aristocratic, and very quiet, with beautiful rooms and large suites. It has long been the choice of foreign diplomats and wealthy Spanish families. AE, DC, MC, V.

Villa Magna, Paseo de la Castellana 22 (tel. 261 4900). 194 rooms. The most exclusive of hotels and Madrid's international rendezvous. With restaurant, bars, banquet rooms and garage. Decor is elegant and tasteful; pleasant garden. AE, DC.

Deluxe

Alameda, Avda. de Logroño 100 (tel. 747 4800). 143 rooms. Opposite Barajas airport, with free transportation to city. Attractive rooms, but readers have mentioned noise, a gloomy dining room and poor service. With pool. AE, DC, MC, V.

Barajas, Avda. de Logroño (tel. 747 7700). 230 rooms. Close to the airport, a sister hotel to the *Alameda* but rather more expensive. With pool; mini-bars in all rooms. AE, DC, MC, V.

Castellana, Castellana 49 (tel. 410 0200). 311 rooms. Elegant hotel right on the Castellana, just above Piazza Emilio Castelar. AE, DC, MC, V.

Eurobuilding, Padre Damián 23 (tel. 457 1700). 420 rooms. An enormous hotel with two entrances, one on Padre Damián and one on Juan Ramón Jiménez. With a pool, gardens, several bars, nightclub; *Balthasar* restaurant and *Le Relais* coffeeshop. Popular with Americans and businessmen. AE, DC, MC, V.

Holiday Inn, in the Azca Center off Calle Orense (tel. 456 7014). 313 rooms. This latest addition to the Madrid luxury-hotel scene opened in March 1985. Part of the big shopping and entertainment complex close to the Castellana in the north of the city; decor is luxurious, and there is a pool, sauna and gymnasium, executive suites, banqueting salons, conference rooms, underground garage, an Italian-style cafeteria, and a steak house.

Luz Palacio, Paseo de la Castellana 57 (tel. 442 5100). 182 rooms. Tastefully decorated, with restaurants, cocktail lounge, garage, and all amenities. AE, DC, MC, V.

Meliá Castilla, Capitán Haya 43 (tel. 270 8400). 936 rooms. Madrid's largest hotel in the increasingly fashionable and gourmet area in the north of the city. It has a pool, and also boasts the *Scala* nightclub, Madrid's only nightspot of any real standing. AE, DC, MC, V.

Meliá Madrid, Princesa 27 (tel. 241 8200). 266 rooms spread over 25 stories. Elegant and modern, with every convenience, own garage. Recommended. AE, DC, MC, V.

Miguel Angel, Miguel Angel 31 (tel. 442 8199). 305 rooms. Luxurious hotel with elegantly appointed public and private rooms. Conveniently located in smart area, it has fast become a favorite with discerning travelers. Pool. AE, DC, MC, V.

Mindanao, San Francisco de Sales 15 (tel. 449 5500). 289 rooms. In residential area close to the University City in the northwest of the city. With pools and sauna. *Domayo* restaurant offers regional Spanish dishes and French cuisine, while the *Keynes* bar is a favorite spot for Spanish society. AE, DC, MC, V.

Monte Real, Arroyo Fresno 17 (tel. 216 2140). 77 rooms. In the Puerta de Hierro section out of town, and the last word in ritzy elegance, quiet and dignified. With pool and large gardens, and just 1 km. from Puerta de Hierro golf club. AE, DC, MC, V.

Palace, Plaza de las Cortes 7 (tel. 429 7551). 518 rooms. Dignified turn-of-the-century hotel, a slightly down-market step-sister of the nearby *Ritz* and long a favorite of politicians and journalists. Its *belle époque* décor—especially the glass dome over the lounge—is superb, if now somewhat faded in parts—some of the rooms are in need of refurbishing. Very central, opposite parliament and close to the Prado Museum. AE, V.

Princesa Plaza, Princesa 40 (tel. 242 3500). 406 rooms. Modern, functional hotel on busy central avenue, a focal point for Madrid businessmen. AE, DC, MC, V.

Wellington, Velázquez 8 (tel. 275 4400). 257 rooms. An old favorite in the Salamanca district close to Retiro Park, attracting a solid, conservative clientele. It has long been a focal point of the bull-fighting world, and in the May San Isidro festivals plays host to famous toreros, breeders and bullring critics. AE, DC, MC, V.

Expensive

Aitana, Castellana 152 (tel. 250 7107). 111 rooms. A comfortable, modern hotel much favored by businessmen, on the northern reaches of the Castellana close to the Azca Center and the Bernabeu soccer stadium. AE, DC, V.

Alcalá, Alcalá 66 (tel. 435 1060). 153 rooms. Convenient for Retiro Park and Goya shopping area. Good value. AE, DC, MC, V.

Arosa, Calle de la Salud 21 (tel. 232 1600). 126 rooms. Overlooking Gran Vía. Despite a rather dingy outward appearance, readers have praised its charm and helpful, friendly service. AE, DC, MC, V.

Calatrava, Tutor 1 (tel. 241 9880). 99 rooms. With disco, private garage. Close to Plaza de España. AE, DC, MC, V.

Chamartín, above Chamartín station (tel. 733 6200). 378 rooms. Large, modern hotel, part of the huge government-financed Chamartín complex. Its size makes it rather impersonal, and it is a long way from the center, though convenient for the station. AE, DC, MC, V.

El Coloso, Leganitos 13 (tel. 248 7600). 53 rooms. Modern, well-appointed hotel, centrally located just off Gran Vía and Plaza España. AE, DC, MC, V.

Convención, O'Donnell 53 (tel. 247 6800). 790 rooms. A huge hotel, opened in 1978 and near Goya shopping area. Self-service cafeteria, direct-dial phones. AE, DC, MC, V.

Cuzco, Castellana 133 (tel. 456 0600). 330 rooms. Modern and pleasant, close to the Bernabeu stadium. AE, DC, MC, V.

Emperador, Gran Vía 53 (tel. 247 2800). 231 rooms. Popular, comfortable, older hotel on corner of San Bernardo. Rooftop pool and terrace with good views. AE, DC, MC, V.

Emperatriz, Lopez de Hoyos 4 (tel. 413 6511). 170 rooms. Attractive, stylish hotel just off the Castellana. Good service; recommended. AE, DC, MC, V.

Escultor, Miguel Angel 3 (tel. 410 4203). 82 rooms. Beautiful, luxurious apartments, just off the Castellana, but geared rather to businessmen and tour groups. AE, DC, MC, V.

Los Galgos, Claudio Coello 139 (tel. 262 4227). 359 rooms. Comfortable; rooms well-appointed and most with balcony. Near Serrano shopping area. AE, DC, MC, V.

Gran Atlanta, Comandante Zorita 34 (tel. 253 5900). 180 rooms. Recent, functional hotel close to the Azca Center on Orense. Decor is dark and gloomy in typically Spanish style, but the hotel is comfortable and the service friendly. AE, DC, MC, V.

Gran Hotel Velázquez, Velázquez 62 (tel. 275 2800). 130 rooms. Oldish, but comfortable and spacious with some style, though it has begun to take tour groups. It is a regular venue for Madrileños, who favor its banqueting rooms for their weddings, while its bar frequently hosts one of the few remaining teatime *tertulias*. AE, DC, MC, V.

MADRID

Gran Hotel Versalles, Covarrubias 4 (tel. 447 5700). 96 rooms. Small, quiet hotel with regular clientele, near Alonso Martínez. AE, DC, V.

Liabeny, Salud 3 (tel. 232 5306). 158 rooms. Modern, functional hotel, centrally located on Plaza del Carmen, close to shops, Gran Vía and Puerta del Sol. AE, MC, V.

Mayorazgo, Flor Baja 3 (tel. 247 2600). 200 rooms. Pleasant hotel tucked away in a side street off Gran Vía. AE, DC, MC, V.

Menfis, Gran Vía 74 (tel. 247 0900). 122 rooms. Pleasant '60s-style hotel, popular with foreigners for its central location on Gran Vía close to Plaza España. AE, DC, V.

Plaza, Plaza de España (tel. 247 1200). 306 rooms. Elegant, central hotel very popular with Americans and Germans. With pool. AE, DC, MC, V.

Suecia, Marqués de Casa Riera 4 (tel. 231 6900). 64 rooms. Once patronized by Hemingway, this hotel boasts a good Scandinavian restaurant. Close to Cibeles and next to the Teatro Bellas Artes just off Alcalá. Mixed reports from readers. AE, DC, MC, V.

Moderate

Anaco, Tres Cruces 3 (tel. 222 4604). 37 rooms. Small, modern and comfortable hotel just off Plaza del Carmen. Very central. AE, DC, MC, V.

Carlos V, Maestro Vitoria 5 (tel. 231 4100). 67 rooms. Pleasant old hotel, centrally located just off main shopping street. AE, DC, MC, V.

Colón, Dr. Esquerdo 117 (tel. 274 6800). 385 rooms. Large 4-star hotel with good rates, though a little out of the center. AE, DC, MC, V.

Gran Vía, Gran Vía 25 (tel. 222 1121). 163 rooms. Long-standing favorite of foreign visitors for its central location on Montera and Gran Vía. Shabby exterior but fully renovated inside. AE, DC, MC, V.

Inglés, Echegaray 10 (tel. 429 6551). 58 rooms. A good, small hotel located in the older part of the city near Puerta del Sol. AE, DC, MC, V.

Marquina, Prim 11 (tel. 222 9010). 21 rooms. Apartment hotel, small, modern and comfortable, just off Paseo Recoletos. Reader-recommended.

Moderno, Arenal 2 (tel. 231 0900). 98 rooms. Renovated old hotel in a very central position just off Puerta del Sol. Traffic can be noisy. AE, V.

Opera, Cuesta Santo Domingo 2 (tel. 241 2800). 81 rooms. In the old part of the city close to the Opera and only a short walk from the Royal Palace.

Principe Pío, Cuesta San Vicente 14 (tel. 247 8000). 157 rooms. Pleasant hotel near the Royal Palace and North station. Good service. AE, MC, V.

Regina, Alcalá 19 (tel. 221 4725). 142 rooms. Elegant, older hotel, very central, opposite Calle Sevilla. AE, V.

Rex, Gran Vía 43 (tel. 247 4800). 146 rooms. Good, smallish hotel on corner of Silva, just down from Callao. AE, DC, V.

Tirol, Marqués de Urquijo 4 (tel. 248 1900). 93 rooms. Situated just off Princesa not far from Parque del Oeste. Its bar is famous for its cocktails. V.

Victoria, Plaza del Angel 7 (tel. 231 4500). 110 rooms. Stylish old hotel with stained-glass windows and decorative cupola, pleasantly located between Plaza Santa Ana and Plaza del Angel. Long a favorite of bullfighters and aficionados. AE, DC, MC, V.

Zurbano, Zurbano 81 (tel. 441 5500). 262 rooms. Modern, elegant hotel in a fashionable area. High standards. AE, MC, V.

Inexpensive

Alexandra, San Bernardo 29 (tel. 242 0400). 69 rooms. Fairly central. AE, V.

Andorra, Gran Vía 33 (tel. 232 3116). Recently opened and fully-renovated hostel on the 7th floor, close to Plaza Callao. Rooms are quiet despite the central location, and all have fully-equipped bathrooms. Run by a friendly couple who speak some English, and reader-recommended. v.

Asturias, Sevilla 2 (tel. 429 6670). 144 rooms. Old-world charm, but on a rather busy intersection overlooking Plaza Canalejas, just up from Puerta del Sol. Much-needed renovations are underway—check your room is one of those already refurbished before booking. AE, V.

Clíper, Chinchilla 6 (tel. 231 1700). 52 rooms. Good-value hotel on a narrow street off the central part of Gran Vía, between Callao and Red de San Luis. AE, MC, V.

Francisco I, Arenal 15 (tel. 248 0204). 58 rooms. Old hotel with modernized decor, halfway between Puerta del Sol and the Opera. Top-floor restaurant is recommended.

Internacional, Arenal 19 (tel. 248 1800). 74 rooms. Old-world charm and friendly service. Some rooms are excellent, others frankly rather scruffy. DC, MC, V.

Lar, Valverde 16 (tel. 221 6592). 80 rooms. A 3-star hotel with good-value rates. Centrally located, but on an old, somewhat noisy street to the north of Gran Vía. AE, DC, V.

París, Alcalá 2 (tel. 221 6496). 114 rooms. A delightful hotel full of stylish, old-fashioned appeal. Right on Puerta del Sol. DC, V.

Regente, Mesonero Romanos 9 (tel. 221 2941). 124 rooms. Simple, old-fashioned hotel close to Gran Vía and the pedestrian shopping streets of Callao. Good value. AE, MC, V.

Motels

Los Angeles (M), on the N-IV to Andalusia (tel. 696 3815). 46 rooms. 14 km. from town. With pool and tennis.

Avion (M), Avda. Aragón 345 (tel. 747 6222). 64 rooms. 14 km. out of town. Convenient for those driving in from Barcelona.

Los Olivos (M), on the N-IV to Andalusia (tel. 695 6700). 100 rooms. 12 km. out of town. With pool. Reader recommended.

Youth Hostels. There are two youth hostels in Madrid: the biggest is **Richard Schirrmann,** in Casa del Campo park (tel. 463 5699), with 120 beds; the other, more central, one is **Santa Cruz de Marcenado,** at No. 28 on the street of the same name (tel. 247 4532), with 78 beds. The nearest metro to the former is Lago, to the latter it's Argüelles, San Bernardo or Ventura Rodriguez.

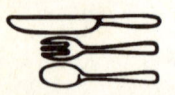

RESTAURANTS. If Madrid is your first stop in Spain, you may feel ravenous before you see any signs of food on the way. Normal meal hours in the capital are even later than in the rest of Spain—where they are already later than elsewhere in Europe! Few people think of eating lunch in the capital before 2 P.M., 3 P.M. is quite normal, and 3.30 not at all unusual; and while most Spanish diners begin to eat at 9.30 or 10, 10.30 is more usual for Madrileños. However, if you just can't wait, a few restaurants and most hotels open their dining rooms earlier for the benefit of foreigners, or you can get a snack in any of the numerous cafeterias around town.

Madrid is plentifully provided with restaurants of all classes and of all types. The truly cosmopolitan mix includes French, German, Italian, Chinese, Mexican, Latin American, Japanese, Moroccan, Polish, Russian and American cuisine—not to mention Asturian, Basque, Galician, Valencian, Catalan, as well, of course, as Castilian.

MADRID

All restaurants, except those in the top 4– and 5–fork classifications, are theoretically required to offer a *menu del día* (although not all of them do, and the practice is becoming less and less common), comprising a 3-course, fixed-price set meal, including bread, wine and dessert. Though there is often a choice, unless the fixed meal happens to be exactly what you want, you may well prefer to compound your own *menu*—though this is almost certain to prove more expensive.

A word of warning: many of the best-known restaurants close for a month in summer, and some are also closed in Easter week. Many close on Sundays, and some also on one other day during the week; be sure to check.

For an approximate guide to prices, see page 21.

Deluxe

El Amparo, Puigcerdá 8 (entrance Jorge Juan 10) (tel. 431 6456). Elegant restaurant with the emphasis on Basque traditional and *nouvelle cuisine.* Imaginative dishes and pleasing decor. Closed Sat. lunch, Sun., Easter week and Aug. AE, V.

Clara's, Arrieta 2 (tel. 242 0071). Superb food in the classic setting of a fine old building on the corner of Plaza Isabel II. Is considered one of the very best gourmet attractions in town. Closed Sun. V.

Club 31, Alcalá 58 (tel. 221 6622). International cuisine and Spanish regional dishes. Under same management as *Jockey* and with same high standards. Ideal for late diners as orders are taken uptil midnight. Closed Aug. AE, DC, V.

Horcher, Alfonso XII 6 (tel. 222 0731). One of Madrid's most famous—and expensive—restaurants. Service is excellent, ladies are even brought a cushion to rest their feet on! Specialties are Central European dishes and game. Closed Sun. AE.

Jockey, Amador de los Ríos 6 (tel. 419 2435). A long-standing favorite and one of the best. Closed Sun. and Aug. AE, DC, MC, V.

Ritz Hotel, Paseo del Prado 5 (tel. 221 2857). A considerable part of the six million dollars recently spent on renovating the Ritz went on refurbishing the dining room, which is now resplendent with silk curtains and marble columns. The hotel garden is probably the most attractive place to dine in summer, and there have been many delighted reports from readers. AE, DC, MC, V.

Zalacaín, Alvarez de Baena 4 (tel. 261 4840). Considered Spain's best restaurant by gourmets. In a private villa with elegant decor and topnotch food; highest recommendations. Closed Sat. lunch, Sun., Easter week and Aug. AE.

Expensive

Al-Mounia, Recoletos 5 (tel. 435 0828). One of the best restaurants in Madrid. Moroccan specialties and an oriental tearoom. Closed Sun., Mon. lunch, and in Aug. AE, DC.

Bajamar, Gran Vía 78 (tel. 248 5903). Offers some of the best seafood in town in its downstairs dining room, but watch those prices. AE, DC, MC, V.

Balthasar, Juan Ramón Jiménez 8 (tel. 457 9191). Elegant restaurant with classical decor and good food. Closed Sun., and in Easter week and Aug. AE, DC, MC, V.

El Bodegón, Pinar 15 (tel. 262 8844). Small restaurant with outstanding food and a regular, faithful clientele. Closed Sun. and in Aug. AE, DC, MC, V.

Cabo Mayor, Juan Hurtado de Mendoza 11 (tel. 250 8776). Imaginative cuisine. Closed Sun. and in Aug. AE, DC, V.

Café de Oriente, Plaza de Oriente 2 (tel. 241 3974). Stylish restaurant. In summer, you can dine on a terrace overlooking the Teatro Real and the Royal Palace. Closed Sat. lunch, Sun. and Aug. AE, DC, V.

MADRID

Las Cuatro Estaciones, General Ibáñez Ibero 5 (tel. 253 6305). For a fixed price, you have a choice of four menus, one for each season of the year, though dishes can be interchanged. Sumptuous decor to match the seasons. A novel and highly recommended restaurant. Closed Sat. and Sun., and in Aug. AE, DC, V.

Escuadrón, Tamayo y Baus 8 (tel. 419 2830). Small, intimate and exclusive. Wonderful game in season. Impeccable food and service. AE, DC, MC, V.

El Gran Chambelán, Ayala 46 (tel. 431 7745). Elegant restaurant with superb cuisine. Try their *menu estrecho y largo,* literally "narrow and wide"—a little of everything, it's delicious. AE, V.

Gure Etxea, Plaza de la Paja 12 (tel. 265 6149). An excellent Basque restaurant, much praised by readers. Closed in Aug. AE, DC, V.

Itxaso, Capitán Haya 58 (tel. 450 6412). Basque restaurant with elegant, somber decor, close to Hotel Meliá Castilla. Its fish and seafood dishes are outstanding. Closed Sun. AE, DC, MC, V.

Korynto, Preciados 36 (tel. 221 5965). A long-established seafood restaurant in the heart of Madrid. Prices are high but the freshness and quality are tops. AE, DC, MC, V.

Lhardy, San Jerónimo 8 (tel. 221 3385). A veritable old Madrid institution. Worth a visit as much for its old-world decor as for its long-famed cuisine. Closed Sun. and in Aug.

Nicolasa, Velázquez 150 (tel. 261 9985). Top Basque dishes served by owners of its namesake in San Sebastián. The decor is most attractive and the waitresses wear Basque costume. AE, DC, MC, V.

O'Pazo, Reina Mercedes 20 (tel. 253 2333). An elegant Galician restaurant with a reputation for some of the best seafood in Madrid. Closed Sun.

El Pescador, José Ortega y Gasset 75 (tel. 402 1290). Prime-quality fish dishes and good service. Closed Sun. and mid-Aug. through mid-Sept.

Platerías, Plaza Santa Ana 11 (tel. 429 7048). Superb dishes in lovely setting on this delightful square. Daily specials are recommended. Closed Sun. and Aug.

Los Porches, Pintor Rosales 1 (tel. 247 7053). Set right in Parque del Oeste, near Plaza España, it features international dishes served in a spacious dining room or—in summer—a large garden. AE, DC, MC, V.

Príncipe de Viana, Manuel de Falla 5 (tel. 259 1448). Fashionable restaurant with Basque, Navarre and international dishes. Closed Sat. lunch, Sun., Easter week and Aug. AE, DC, MC, V.

Sacha, Juan Hurtado de Mendoza 11 (tel. 457 7200). Cozy, with exquisite decor; outdoor dining in summer. AE, V.

Solchaga, Plaza de Alonso Martínez 2 (tel. 447 1496). Owned by a well-known TV personality, this currently very popular dining place resembles an old-fashioned lounge in a private house rather than a restaurant. Closed Sat. lunch and Sun. AE, DC, MC, V.

La Trainera, Lagasca 60 (tel. 435 8954). A good, reliable fish and seafood restaurant with a regular clientele. Closed Sun. and Aug.

Wallis, Raimundo Fernández Villaverde 65 (tel. 456 7170). Both decor and cuisine are exquisite. Reader-recommended. AE, DC, MC, V.

Moderate

Alkalde, Jorge Juan 10 (tel. 276 3359). Cave-like rooms, pleasant atmosphere, excellent food and service. One of Madrid's most consistently good restaurants. AE, DC, V.

Balzac, Moreto 7 (tel. 239 1922). Serves its own original style of Basque cuisine, and is especially well-known for its desserts. Closed Sat. lunch and Sun. AE, V.

MADRID

Casablanca, Barquillo 29 (tel. 221 1568). Popular and original restaurant where you can dine till 1 A.M. Closed Sat. lunch. AE, DC, MC, V.

Casa Botín, Cuchilleros 17 (tel. 266 4217). Just off Plaza Mayor, this is Madrid's oldest restaurant, having been catering to diners since 1725. It was a great favorite with Hemingway, and though popular with Spaniards, too, it is definitely aimed at tourists. Service is pleasant and efficient, the food reasonably good—and, though it has become a tourist mecca, it is still worth a visit. Two sittings for dinner, at 8 and at 10.30; booking essential. AE, DC, MC, V.

Casa Lucio, Cava Baja 35 (tel. 265 8217). Atmospheric restaurant near Plaza Mayor, serving topnotch Spanish fare (steaks, lamb, eel, etc.) in mesón setting in a maze of small rooms. Personalized service, excellent value. Closed Sat. lunch and Aug. AE, DC, V.

Casa Paco, Puerto Cerrada 11 (tel. 266 3166). This atmospheric old tavern is a perennial favorite and renowned for its steaks. Limited space and there is nearly always a line. Closed Sun. and Aug. DC, V.

Las Cuevas de Luis Candelas, Cuchilleros 1 (tel. 266 5428). Another atmospheric place, this one built inside part of the old walls of the city, at the foot of steps leading out of Plaza Mayor. A bit of a tourist trap but fun. AE, DC, MC, V.

El Cosaco, Alfonso VI 4 (tel. 265 3548). Russian restaurant with charming old Russian decor. Open evenings only except Sun. lunch. DC.

Edelweiss, Jovellanos 6 (tel. 221 0326), just behind the Cortes. Substantial portions of German food served. Opens for dinner at 7; reservations are not accepted, so best go early. Closed Sun. and in Aug. AE, MC, V.

Fado, Plaza de San Martín 2 (tel. 231 8924). Portuguese food and singing.

La Gran Tasca, Ballesta 1 (tel. 231 0044). An old standby frequented by many famous figures. Don't be put off by the insalubrious surroundings, inside it's cozy and delightful, and the food is delicious. Closed Sun., July. and Aug. AE, DC, MC, V.

Hogar Gallego, Plaza Comandante Morenas 3 (tel. 248 6404). Galician restaurant specializing in seafood. Outdoor dining in summer. Closed Sun. evening, and most of Aug.

House of Ming, Castellana 74 (tel. 261 9827). Excellent Chinese delicacies served up in a luxurious setting. Closed Aug. AE, DC, V.

Mesón del Corregidor, Plaza Mayor 8 (tel. 266 3024). Touristy but pleasant.

Mesón de San Javier, Conde 3 (tel. 248 0925). Nicely tucked away in a corner behind the City Hall. Good roast pork and lamb. Downstairs is a typical bodega, upstairs a cozy restaurant.

Pepe Botella, Plaza Dos de Mayo (tel. 222 5278). Atmospheric French restaurant named after the unpopular Joseph Bonaparte. In the heart of Madrid's nightlife district.

Sixto Gran Mesón, Cervantes 28 (tel. 468 6602). Excellent food in typical setting. Specialties are roasts and Avilan lamb, but also does good seafood. Closed Sun. evening. AE, DC, MC, V.

Los Siete Jardines, San Vicente Ferrer 86 (tel. 232 2519). Vogue restaurant in Malasaña with "Four Seasons" menus. Atmospheric turn-of-the-century decor with candles, coat-stands, etc.

La Taberna del Alabardero, Felipe V 6 (tel. 241 5192). Alongside the Teatro Real, this stylish restaurant—again, with turn-of-the-century decor—has proved something of a breakthrough in Madrid restaurant traditions. Basque dishes. Closed late-Aug. AE, DC, V.

La Taberna del Prado, Marqués de Cuba (tel. 429 6041). Family-run restaurant with original menu and excellent food. Reader-recommended.

MADRID

La Toja, Siete de Julio 3 (tel. 266 4664). Just off Plaza Mayor and specializing in seafood. A good place to try paella. Opens for dinner at 8. AE, DC, V.

Valentín, San Alberto 3 (tel. 221 1638). Longtime rendezvous of the influential and the famous, from bullfighters to literati. Intimate decor, good service, standard Spanish dishes. Close to Puerta del Sol. AE, DC, MC, V.

Zarauz, Fuentes 13 (tel. 247 7270). Just off Calle Arenal, this one serves a great variety of wonderful seafood plus Basque specialties. Closed Sun. evening, Mon., and mid-July through mid-Sept. AE, DC, MC, V.

Inexpensive

La Argentina, Válgame Diós 9 (tel. 221 3763). Attractive decor and very popular—you may have to wait in the bar. Recommended are its vegetables *gratinados* and its Argentinian specialties. Closed Mon. and Aug.

La Biótica, on Amor de Diós, near Antón Martin metro. Good vegetarian spot. Open for lunch and dinner.

La Bola, Bola 5 (tel. 247 6930). Plenty of old-world charm in this atmospheric restaurant that has been in the same family since the early 1800s. Closed Sun.

El Buda Feliz, Tudescos 5 (tel. 232 4475). Excellent Chinese restaurant near Plaza Callao, recommended by readers.

Casa Ciriaco, Mayor 84 (tel. 248 0620). An atmospheric old standby where the Madrid of 50 years ago lives on. Closed Wed. and in Aug.

Casa Domingo, Alcalá 99 (tel. 226 1895). Opposite the Retiro, for unpretentious sidewalk lunching. Meat dishes from northern Spain.

Casa Ricardo, Fernando el Católico 31 (tel. 446 0100). Open for lunch only. One of Madrid's oldest *tabernas,* boasting bullfighting decor and excellent home-cooking.

El Granero de Lavapies, on Calle Argumosa, near Lavapies metro. Vegetarian restaurant, open for lunch weekdays, and in the evenings at weekends.

El Luarqués, Ventura de la Vega 16 (tel. 429 6174). Decorated with photos of the picturesque port of Luarca on the north coast, this popular restaurant is always packed with Madrileños who recognize its sheer good value. *Fabada asturiana* and *arroz con leche* among the Asturian specialties on the menu. Closed Sun. evening, Mon., and in Aug.

Paris, Huertas 66. Decoration is sparse but clean. Attracts a lively neighborhood clientele. Reader-recommended.

Terra a Nosa, Cava San Miguel 3 (tel. 247 1175). Typical Galician bistro near Plaza Mayor. Popular and crowded, with bags of atmosphere.

Outside Madrid

The following are all (E) and ideally suited for dinner on a summer's evening:

El Mesón, 13 km. (eight miles) out on C607, the road to Colmenar Viejo (tel. 734 1019). In an attractive rustic setting.

Porto Novo, on the N-VI to Galicia, about ten km. (six miles) from Madrid (tel. 207 0173). Closed Sun. night and Mon. AE, DC, V.

Rancho Texano, Avda. de Aragón 364 (tel. 747 4744). On the N-II, the road to the airport and Barcelona, 12 km. (seven miles). An old favorite specializing in grilled steaks. Closed Sun. evening. AE, DC, MC, V.

Los Remos, on the N-VI to Galicia, 12 km. (seven miles). A longtime favorite with Madrileños. Superb fish and seafood, and some meat dishes too. This one is the best. Closed Sun. evening and last 2 weeks in Aug. V.

CAFETERIAS. For snacks a good place to go is one of the numerous cafeterias—by which we do not mean the self-service type of establishment found in the United States and Britain, but rather, smart cafes with table service. Here,

MADRID

you can order sandwiches, pastries, even simple meals, *platos combinados*, etc., and drink from a choice of fruit juices and other soft drinks, coffee—as well as beer, wine and liquor. Cafeterias are open from early in the morning until at least midnight. They are the best place for breakfast and mid-morning coffee, or for a meal outside restaurant hours. Reliable chains with branches all over Madrid are **California, Manila, Morrison** and **Nebraska.**

TRADITIONAL CAFES. Cafe Comercial, Glorieta de Bilbao 7. An old-time cafe that has not changed much over the last three decades; always crowded.

Cafe Gijón, Paseo de Recoletos 21. The best and most famous of the remaining cafes of old. It is still a hangout for writers and artists, carrying on a tradition dating back to the turn of the century, when the cafe was a meeting place of the literati. Tables outside on the main avenue in summer.

Cafe Lyon, Alcalá 57. Charming, old-fashioned decor; just up from Cibeles.

Cafe Metropolitano, Glorieta de Cuatro Caminos. Student atmosphere.

Cafe Viena, Luisa Fernanda 23. Done out like an old-time cafe; you can dine here evenings to the accompaniment of piano music.

The Embassy, corner of Castellana and Ayala. Elegant pastry shop and tearoom with a vast assortment of sandwiches, canapés and pastries.

La Mallorquina, on Puerta del Sol between Mayor and Arenal. An old-world pastry shop with a tea salon, where the incredible, probably doomed, tea ritual is enacted between 6 and 7 P.M.

FAST FOOD. American hamburger joints such as **McDonalds, Burger King** and **Wendy** have mushroomed in Madrid over the last few years, and can now be found all over the city. In some cases, they have been obliged to keep to the traditional Spanish decor, which makes for some interesting not to say bizarre juxtapositions—the McDonalds on the corner of Montera and Gran Vía, and the Burger King on Arenal just off Puerta del Sol, are especially worth seeing. **Pizza Hut** also has a couple of branches, at Orense 11 and Plaza Santa Barbara 8. **VIPS** is a chain of trendy Spanish cafeterias very popular with the young of Madrid, and serving hamburgers; branches at Velázquez 78 and 136, Julián Romea 4, Paseo de la Habana 17, and Princesa 5.

Self Service. A particularly good chain of self-service restaurants offering typically Spanish food in clean, pleasant surroundings is **Topics,** with branches at Princesa 5, Fuencarral 126, Puerta del Sol 14, Plaza Mostenses 11 (just off Gran Vía), and Núñez de Balboa 75.

BARS AND CAFES. If you want to spend an enjoyable, typically Spanish, evening, then go bar-hopping in any of the following areas. You'll find many bars and cafes where you can sample the local wine, or have a glass of beer, and choose from any number of tapas. Stylish cafes with old-time piano music or chamber music are also very much in vogue, as are jazz cafes.

The **Malasaña** area around Bilbao, Fuencarral and San Bernardo is the "in" place for Madrid's youth, students and hippies. There are countless lively, trendy bars open till the small hours around Plaza Dos de Mayo and Calles Ruiz, San Andrés and Vicente Ferrer. The following are just a few suggestions:

Cafe Comercial, Glorieta de Bilbao. This old-time cafe is a popular rendezvous for the Malasaña area.

Cafe de Ruíz, Ruíz 14. A popular cafe with *belle époque* decor, potted palms, hat-stands, etc., and offering Brazilian music and lots of life.

Cafe de Silverio, Manuela Malasaña. Flamenco can often be enjoyed here evenings, Thursday through Sunday.

Crêperie Ma Bretagne, San Vicente Ferrer 9. Specializes in sweet and savory crêpes. Open till 1 A.M.; closed Sun.

Mala Saña, San Vicente Ferrer 23. Trendy disco-cum-cafe with disco dance floor, loud music, vogue decor, and no entrance charge.

Manuela, San Vicente Ferrer 29, just off Plaza Dos de Mayo. Atmospheric cafe with live jazz.

Tetería de la Abuela, Espíritu Santo 19. "Granny's Teapot," with 30 different teas and herbal drinks. Very popular.

The **Huertas** area around Calle de las Huertas, leading from Paseo del Prado to Plaza del Angel, is another lively nighttime locale chockablock with cafes offering folk or chamber music and several colorful tapa bars.

El Elhecho, on Calle Huertas. Very popular. Turn-of-the-century decor with potted ferns *(elhechos);* evenings there's chamber or piano music.

La Fídula, Huertas 57. Another stylish cafe with (usually chamber) music nightly at 11.

Salon del Prado, Prado 4. Chamber music every night at 11. Open 1.30 P.M. to 2 A.M.

The **Orense** development around the Azca Center has proved a magnet for the teenagers and the young of Madrid, who congregate here in the evenings in the many fast-food joints, discos, *whiskerías* and *coctelerías*. It is perhaps not worth making a special trip to, but if your hotel happens to be in the area, and you are young—or young at heart—then you could do worse than take a look.

The traditional mesones area just off **Plaza Mayor** on Cava San Miguel and Calle Cuchilleros has long been famous. Do the rounds of the mesones with names like the **Tortilla, Champiñón, Gamba, Cochinillo,** etc., most of them named after their particular specialty, and on a busy night you may well come across someone playing the guitar and singing, or be serenaded by the wandering *tuna* minstrels.

For some of the oldest bars in Madrid, try the streets around the **Rastro.** Here you'll find such durable retreats as the **Mesón de Paredes, Jesús y María, Magdalena, Cascorro,** and **La Esquinita**—the latter, a bar with magnificent tapas, beer served in mugs, and roast chicken. The **Taverna de Antonio Sánchez,** at Mesón de Paredes 13, is an old mesón just off Plaza de Tirso de Molina, that first opened its doors in 1850 and was once a hangout for bullfighters. Its decor includes the head of the bull that killed Antonio Sánchez, son of the owner, and some drawings by Zuloaga.

The old, narrow streets between **Puerta del Sol** and **Plaza Santa Ana** are packed with crowded, colorful tapa bars. Wander along Espoz y Mina, Victoria, Cruz, Núñez de Arce, and Echegaray, and enter any bar that takes your fancy. Don't miss out on the alleyway, Pasaje Matheu, between Victoria and Espoz y Mina, where there are several favorites. Here are but a handful of the many places on offer:

Cafe Central, Plaza del Angel 10. Atmospheric, old-style cafe with jazz, folk and classical music. Often has live jazz between 10 and midnight.

Cervecería Alemana, Plaza Santa Ana 6. Popular beer hall over 100 years old, originally founded by Germans. Once patronized by (who else?!) Hemingway, and now by tourists.

La Chuleta, on Manuel Fernández y González. An inviting display of tapas—and tables for the weary to sit down at and rest their legs. Try the pork chops *(chuletas)* or baby eel *(angullas)*.

MADRID

Cuevas de Sésamo, Príncipe 7. Popular basement piano bar.

La Trucha, Manuel Fernández y González 3. Colorful and atmospheric, with strings of garlic and giant hams hanging from the ceiling. Specialties are *trucha navarra,* trout stuffed with ham and garlic, and *rabo del toro,* bull's tail.

Viva Madrid, Manuel Fernández y González 7. Open from midday till 1.30 A.M. for chess washed down with Irish coffee.

NIGHTLIFE. Since Franco's death, the nightclub scene in Madrid has flung off all restraint and the city now throbs with shows featuring striptease, topless dancers, drag and every kind of no-holds-barred entertainment. Pick-up bars, ranging from the old-time standbys to flashy, elegant new places in the northern Castellana area, have multiplied enormously over recent years. Travelers who knew the tame Spain of a few years ago will be amazed by the change—all censorship has been discarded.

Cleofas, Goya 7 (tel. 276 4523). Disco, followed by orchestra, dancing, and, at 1 A.M., a show—though the latter will likely be lost on anyone whose Spanish is not very good. Closed Mon.

Florida Park, in Retiro Park (tel. 273 7804). You can have dinner here, and the shows often feature ballet or Spanish dance. Open from 9.30 to 3.30 in the morning, daily except Sun. and Mon., with shows at 11.

Madrid's Casino, 28 km. (17 miles) out, on the N–VI road to La Coruña, at Torrelodones (tel. 859 0312). One of the largest casinos in Europe and offering French and American roulette, chemin de fer, baccarat, and blackjack. Three restaurants, six bars, and a nightclub with cabaret.

La Scala, Rosario Pino 7, in Hotel Meliá Castilla (tel. 450 4500). Madrid's top nightclub, with dinner, dancing and cabaret at 8.30, and a second, less expensive, show at 12.45. Open till 4 A.M.

Windsor, Raimundo Fernández Villaverde 65 (tel. 455 5814). On corner of the Castellana. Dancing from 11.30 with a show at 1 A.M. Recommended. Closed Mon.

Xairo, Paz 11 (tel. 231 2440). Dancing and music hall shows on Sat.

Xenon, Plaza Callao (tel. 231 9794). Dancing to orchestra from 11.30 and cabaret at 1 A.M. Beneath Callao movie theater.

Discos. These are numerous and very popular in Madrid. Some charge an entrance fee, usually starting around 1,000 ptas., which includes your first drink; others just charge for your drinks. Gay discos and transvestite clubs are also thick on the ground. For a complete listing, read the weekly *Guía del Ocio.* The following are just a few of the better-known ones:

Joy Eslava, Arenal 11. Located in the old Teatro Eslava, and one of the liveliest and most popular discos in Madrid.

Macumba, Chamartín station. Open Wed. to Sun. with live shows most nights; closes at 3 A.M.

Mississippi, Princesa 45. One of the most popular, with German beer on tap and meals till 5 A.M.

Pacha, Barceló 11. Another leading contender on the disco scene. Opened in 1980 in the old Teatro Barcelo; decorated like Studio 54 in New York. Open Wed. to Sun. only.

Marquee, and **Rock Ola,** Padre Xifre 5. *The* place to go for the latest sounds: Marquee favors hard rock, Rock Ola new wave. Live bands.

Zacarias, Miguel Angel 29, in Hotel Miguel Angel. Where the smart set go.

MADRID

Flamenco. Madrid has some of the best flamenco shows in the country. Some of the clubs serve dinner, though you can choose just to watch the show and have a drink. Dining is expensive, around 4,000–5,500 ptas. a head, but it ensures the best seats. If you are not dining, entrance including one drink varies between 1,500–2,000 ptas. Clubs serving dinner usually open around 9 or 9.30, those offering show only at around 11 P.M. Most clubs stay open until 2 or 3 A.M. Be sure to reserve.

Arco de Cuchilleros, Cuchilleros 7 (tel. 266 5867). Small, intimate club in the heart of old Madrid, just off Plaza Mayor. One of the cheapest and the show is good. No dining. Open 10.30–2.30 with two shows nightly.

Los Cabales, Felipe III 4 (tel. 266 2880). Between Calle Mayor and Plaza Mayor, this is the one visited by most tour groups. Open from 10.30 P.M.

Café de Chinitas, Torija 7 (tel. 248 5135). Well-known throughout Spain and abroad with some famous *cuadros*. This one serves dinner. The show is good and so is the food. Open 9–3.

Los Canasteros, Barbieri 10 (tel. 231 8163). Show and drinks only, no dinner. Open 11–3.30.

Corral de la Morería, Morería 17 (tel. 265 8446). One of the best, owned by the famous Lucero Tena. Serves dinner. Open 9–3.

Corral de la Pacheca, Juan Ramón Jiménez 26 (tel. 458 1113). Right up in the northern part of town. A bit touristy but fun. Folk dancing as well as flamenco. Dinner prices are modest (around 3,000 ptas.). Open 9.30–2.

Torres Bermejas, Mesonero Romanos 11 (tel. 232 3322). Another good one for serious flamenco, though the later show may not appeal to the uninitiated. Offers a choice of three dinner menus, or you can go to the later show and just have a drink. Open 9.30–2.30.

Venta del Gato, Avda. de Burgos 214 (tel. 202 3427). Seven km. (four miles) north on the road to Burgos. Authentic flamenco, and other flamenco dancers among the audience. The show begins at 11.30.

CITY TOURS. Tours of Madrid are run by the following three tour operators: *Pullmantur,* Plaza de Oriente 8 (tel. 241 1807); *Trapsatur,* San Bernardo 23 (tel. 241 4407); and *Juliá Tours,* Gran Vía 68 (tel. 248 9605). All three offer the same tours at the same prices and there is little to choose between them. In high season all tours (except bullfights) operate daily, but in low season the tours may be shared out among the three operators. Tours are conducted in English as well as Spanish, and if need be, in French and other languages too. You can book your tours direct with the operators at the addresses above, or through any travel agency, or, in most cases, through your hotel. Departure points are from the above addresses, though in some cases you can be collected from your hotel.

Madrid Artístico. Morning tour of Madrid including visits to the Royal Palace and Prado Museum. Entrances included.

Madrid Panorámico. A panoramic drive around the city seeing all the main sights as well as some of the more outlying ones such as the University City, Casa del Campo Park, northern reaches of the Castellana and the Bernabeu soccer stadium. This is an ideal orientation drive for the first-time visitor to Madrid. It is a half-day tour, usually in the afternoons.

Madrid de Noche. This night tour of Madrid is available in various combinations. All begin with a drive through the city to see the illuminations of its monuments and fountains, followed either by dinner in a restaurant and a visit to a flamenco club; or by dinner and cabaret at Madrid's leading nightclub, *La Scala;* or by a visit to both a flamenco show and a nightclub.

MADRID

Panorámica y Toros. Departures on days when there are bullfights (usually Sundays) 1½ hours before the fight begins. Panoramic tour of the city seeing the most important sights and an explanation of bullfighting before you arrive at the Ventas bullring to watch the *corrida*.

EXCURSIONS. Whole- or half-day excursions from Madrid to the places listed below are run by *Pullmantur, Trapsatur* and *Juliá Tours*. (For addresses and points of departure, see above under *City Tours*.) Tours can be booked through your hotel, travel agencies or at the tour operators' headquarters. Below we list only those tours which return to Madrid on the same day. Excursions to places further afield or involving overnight stays are also available; apply to any of the three operators for details.

Aranjuez. Half-day excursion in the afternoon, daily except Tues., visiting the Royal Palace, gardens and the Casita del Labrador.

Avila, Segovia, La Granja. Full-day tour driving to Avila to see the medieval city walls, the cathedral and the Convent of Santa Teresa, birthplace of the saint. On to Segovia to see the 2,000-year-old Roman aqueduct, to visit either the cathedral or the alcázar castle, and lunch in a typical restaurant. Return via La Granja, once the summer residence of Spanish kings, to visit the palace and gardens modeled on Versailles. On Mon. the palace of Riofrío will be substituted for La Granja.

Cuenca. Full-day tour, Tues. and Thurs., Apr. through Oct. Visits to the Enchanted City with its strange rock formations, and to the picturesque city of Cuenca, famous for its hanging houses, and where you will see Plaza Mayor, the cathedral, and the Museums of Archeology and Abstract Art. Lunch included. *Pullmantur* only; book in advance.

Escorial and Valley of the Fallen. Full- or half-day excursion, daily except Mon. On the half-day excursion you visit the Monastery of the Escorial, including the mausoleum of the Spanish kings since Charles V, and the Valley of the Fallen built to commemorate those who died in Spain's Civil War of 1936–39 and whose basilica houses the tomb of the dictator General Franco. The full-day excursion includes lunch and a visit to the Casita del Príncipe (Prince's House) at the Escorial.

Rutas Verdes de Madrid. Tours through Madrid's countryside. Two itineraries operate on alternate Sat. The first route takes in the Sierra de Buitrago, the reservoir of Atazar and Torrelaguna, with a lunch stop in Buitrago. The second one covers La Cabrera, Valle de Lozoya, lunch in Rascafria, Puerto de Cotos and Villalba. Buses leave from outside the Tourist Office on Duque de Medinaceli, just off Plaza de las Cortes. *Juliá Tours, Trapsatur.*

Salamanca. Full-day tour, twice weekly on Tues. and Sat. only, in summer. Drive via the medieval walls of Avila to the city of Salamanca where you will visit the ancient and prestigious university, the old and new cathedrals, the convents of San Esteban and Las Dueñas, and Plaza Mayor, the most beautiful plaza in Spain. The trip includes lunch. *Trapsatur* only.

Salamanca and Alba de Tormes. Full-day tour, Wed. and Fri., summer only. Visit Salamanca as previous itinerary above, then on to Alba de Tormes to visit the Carmelite Convent which houses the remains of Santa Teresa of Avila. *Juliá Tours* only; book in advance.

Segovia, La Granja and Riofrío. Full-day excursion, Thurs. and Sun. only, summer. Lunch in Segovia. *Pullmantur* only.

Toledo. Whole- or half-day excursions (morning or afternoon) to this historic city visiting the cathedral, the Chapel of Santo Tomé to see El Greco's *Burial of the Count of Orgaz*, one of the old synagogues, the Church of San Juan de

MADRID

los Reyes, and a sword factory for a demonstration of the typical Toledo damascene work. The full-day tour also includes lunch in a restaurant and a visit to the Hospital de Tavera.

Toledo and Aranjuez. Daily except Tues. Full-day excursion to Toledo visiting places mentioned above (except Tavera), lunch, and on to Aranjuez on the banks of the Tagus, to visit the Royal Palace and the Casita del Labrador, "the laborer's cottage" modeled on the Trianon at Versailles.

Toledo, Escorial and Valley of the Fallen. Full-day excursion, daily except Mon., visiting Toledo (as above), lunch, the monastery of the Escorial and the basilica of the Valley of the Fallen.

MUSEUMS. The opening times given below hold good at time of writing, but are subject to frequent change, so do check before making a journey. Most Madrid museums have different schedules for winter and summer months. *Patrimonio Nacional* (i.e. state-owned) museums are free to Spaniards with I.D., but make an entrance charge to visitors from abroad.

Museo del Aire (Air Museum), ten km. (six miles) out, on Paseo de Extremadura. Collection of planes and mementos illustrating the history of aviation and housed in Escuela de Transmisiones. Open Tues. to Sun. 10–2; closed Mon.

Museo de América (Americas Museum), Reyes Católicos 6. Excellent displays of Inca and Quinbaya treasures. Open Tues. to Sun. 10–2; closed Mon. *Note:* museum has been shut for restorations, so check before making a journey.

Museo Arqueológico Nacional (Archeology Museum), Serrano 13. Admirable collection including some particularly fine Greek vases and Roman artifacts, 180,000 coins, a good ceramics collection, the treasures of Iberian Spain—among them, the famous Dama de Elche and the Dama Ofrente del Cerro de los Santos—and a large display of medieval art and furniture. In its gardens you can visit a replica of the Altamira Caves, of particular interest now that exploration of the original is strictly limited. Open Tues. to Sun. 9–1.30; closed Mon.

Museo de Carruajes (Royal Coach Museum), Paseo Vírgen del Puerto. Can be visited on an individual ticket or on an all-inclusive ticket to the Royal Palace. Open Mon. to Sat., 10–12.45 and 3.30–5.15 in winter, 10–12.45 and 4–5.45 in summer; Sun. and fiestas 10–1.30 only. Closed when official functions taking place in the Royal Palace.

Museo de Cera (Wax Museum), Paseo de Recoletos 41. One of the better examples of this specialized genre, with panels of scenes and personages out of Spanish history, as well as personalities ranging from Gary Cooper to President Kennedy. Open Mon. to Sun. 10.30–1.30 and 4–8.30.

Museo Cerralbo, Ventura Rodríguez 17. Tapestries, paintings, and some of the loveliest old porcelain to be seen anywhere, housed in the Cerralbo mansion. A good place to see the aristocratic setting of a turn-of-the-century villa. Open Tues. to Sat. 10–2 and 4–7, Sun. 10–2; closed Mon. and in Aug.

Museo de Ciencias Naturales (Natural Science Museum), Paseo de la Castellana 80. Zoological, geological and entomological collections. Open Mon. to Sat. 9–2 and 3–6, Sun. and fiestas 10–2.

Museo del Ejército (Army Museum), Méndez Núñez 1. Vast but well-labeled collection of trophies, weapons and documents from wars in Europe and America, with a special section dedicated to the Civil War. Open Tues. to Sat. 10–5, Sun. 10–2; closed Mon.

Museo de Escultura al Aire Libre (Openair Sculpture Museum). Situated beneath the overpass where Juan Bravo meets the Castellana. Contains the well-known *Sirena Varada* by Chillida.

MADRID

Museo Español de Arte Contemporáneo (Museum of Contemporary Spanish Art), Avda. Juan de Herrera in the University City. Modern art and sculpture, with 375 paintings and 200 sculptures—including works by Picasso and Miró—set in pleasant gardens. Open Tues. to Sat. 10–6, Sun. 10–3; closed Mon.

Museo del Ferrocarril (Railroad Museum). In the old Delicias station on Calle del Ferrocarril.

Museo Lázaro Galdiano, Serrano 122. One of the "musts" of Madrid, this museum is housed in an old, aristocratic mansion, and—besides containing a magnificent collection of paintings, furniture, clocks, armor, weapons, jewels, and artifacts—is a delight thanks to the tasteful arrangement of its treasures. There is a sizable collection of English paintings and the best display in Europe of ivory and enamel, as well as works by El Greco, Zurbarán, Velázquez and Goya. Open Tues. to Sun. 10–2; closed Mon.

Museo Municipal (Municipal Museum), Fuencarral 78. Several rooms depicting Madrid's past, including a model of the city as it was in 1830. Open daily 10–2 and 5–9; closed Sun. P.M. and Mon. A.M.

Museo Nacional de Artes Decorativas (National Museum of Decorative Art), Montalbán 12. Interesting collection of Spanish ceramics, gold and silver ornaments, glass, textiles, embroidery, furniture, and domestic utensils. Open Tues. to Fri. 10–5, Sat., Sun. and fiestas 10–2; closed Mon. and July through Sept.

Museo Nacional de Etnología (Ethnological Museum), Alfonso XII 68. Primitive artifacts and weapons from the Philippines, Africa, Asia and America, with several interesting mummies. Open Tues. to Sun. 10–1; closed Mon. and Aug.

Museo Naval (Navy Museum), Montalbán 2. Ship models, nautical instruments, etc., with two rooms dedicated to the Battle of Lepanto and to the Discovery of America. The most famous exhibit is Juan de Cosa's original map, used by Columbus on his first voyage to the New World. Open Tues. to Sun. 10.30–1.30; closed Mon.

Museo del Prado, Paseo del Prado. The Prado is one of the world's greatest art collections. If your time is limited, the most priceless treasures—Velázquez, El Greco, Murillo, Zurbarán and Bosch (though not Goya)—are one floor up and can be reached directly by a flight of steps from the outside, thus bypassing the ground floor and, incidentally, the long lines that often form at the lower entrance. Once inside, you have access to both floors, though not necessarily to special exhibitions which are charged separately. The Prado is always unbearably crowded, especially at weekends. Its modernization program involving the installation of airconditioning and better lighting is now well under way, but until it is completed some works are not on show while others have been moved to temporary locations and may be difficult to find. Open Tues. to Sat. 10–5 (summer 10–6), Sun. 10–2; closed Mon.

Admission to the Prado also includes entrance to the **Cason del Buen Retiro** annex, home of 19th-century Spanish painting and of Picasso's *Guernica* (entrance to latter is round the back in Alfonso XII). If you can't visit both on the same day, hang on to your ticket as it will still be valid for the part you haven't seen. Open same hours as Prado—except Wed., when it's open 3–9.

Museo Romántico (Romantic Museum), San Mateo 13. Designed and decorated like a 19th-century palace with paintings, furnishings and *objets d'art* from 1830–68. Open Tues. to Sat. 10–6, Sun. 10–2; closed Mon. and Aug. through mid-Sept.

Museo Sorolla, General Martínez Campos 37. The famous painter's house with a number of his works, as well as a good collection of popular art and sculpture. Open Tues. to Sun. 10–2; closed Mon.

MADRID

Museo Taurino (Bullfighting Museum), Ventas Bullring at the end of Calle Alcalá. Bullfighting paraphernalia. Open Tues. to Sun. 9–3; closed Mon.

Real Academia de Bellas Artes de San Fernando (Fine Arts Academy), Alcalá 13. A collection of mainly Spanish paintings, including works by Goya, Murillo, Zurbarán, Ribera and Rubens. Open Mon. to Sat. 10–2; closed Sun. and fiestas.

PLACES OF INTEREST. Casa de Lope de Vega, Cervantes 11. The great playwright's house and garden, skilfully restored. Open Tues. to Sun. 11–2; closed Mon. and mid-July through mid-Sept.

Ermita de San Antonio de la Florida and Goya Pantheon, Glorieta de San Antonio de la Florida. The hermitage dates from the end of the 17th century; it was built by order of Charles IV and designed by Churriguera and Sabatini. The ceiling of the church is covered in frescos by Goya of respectable court officials hobnobbing with less respectable ladies, though they are dimly lit. The church is now a kind of museum to Goya, and the artist's headless body is buried here. He died in France in 1828 and 60 years later his body, minus its head, was exhumed and brought to rest in Spain. Open daily 11–1 and 3–6; closed Wed. and Sun. P.M.

Monasterio de las Descalzas Reales, Plaza de las Descalzas Reales 3. A 16th-century convent with superb and lavish ornamentation and a veritable wealth of jewels and religious ornaments, paintings including one by Zurbarán, and famous Flemish tapestries based on designs by Rubens. Part of the building is still used as a convent. The entrance ticket also includes a visit to the Monastery of the Incarnation not far away (see below). Open Mon. to Thurs. 10.30–12.45 and 4–5.15; closed Fri. to Sun. and fiesta P.M.S

Monasterio de la Encarnación, Plaza de la Encarnación. Begun in 1611, this convent contains hundreds of paintings and frescos, but is in fact less interesting than the Descalzas Reales. Open Mon. to Sat. 10.30–1.30 and 4–6; closed Sun. and fiestas.

Palacio de Liria, Princesa 20. Contains an immense wealth of paintings by many great European masters, including Titian and Rembrandt, and a portrait by Goya of the 13th Duchess of Alba, believed to have been the model for his famous paintings in the Prado of *La Maja Vestida* and *La Maja Desnuda.* The palace can be visited by applying in writing in advance. Twelve of its rooms are open to the public. The guide who takes visitors round, though very informative, speaks only Spanish. Open Sat. only; closed Aug.

Palacio de El Pardo, in the village of El Pardo, 15 km. (nine miles) from Madrid. El Pardo is surrounded by woods which were much favored by the kings of Spain as hunting grounds. The palace was begun originally in the 15th century, but was mostly built by Sabatini during the reign of Charles III. It contains works by Titian, Bosch and Coello. The home of Franco from 1940 until his death in 1975, much of it now stands as a museum to that period of Spanish history. Open Mon. to Sat. 10–1 and 4–7, Sun. 10–1.

Palacio Real, Plaza de Oriente. The Royal Palace was begun in the reign of Charles III. Entrance is through the vast courtyard on the left of the palace, and then through the door to the right of the courtyard. Guides are available inside. Admission varies depending on how much you want to see; you can visit just the State Apartments—or buy an all-inclusive ticket that includes the Royal Armory, Royal Library, Royal Pharmaceutical Dispensary and Coach Museum. Open Mon. to Sat., 10–12.45 and 3.30–5.15 in winter, 10–12.45 and 4–5.45 in summer; Sun. and fiestas 10–1.30. The palace is closed to the public when in use for official functions.

MADRID

Real Basílica de San Francisco el Grande, Plaza de San Francisco. Madrid's most outstanding church. Open daily 11–1 and 4–7.

Real Fábrica de Tapices, Fuenterrabiá 2. A visit to the workshops of the Royal Tapestry Factory is recommended, and includes entrance to their exhibition of tapestries. Open Mon. to Fri. 9.30–12.30; closed Sat., Sun., fiestas and Aug.

Temple of Debod, in the Parque del Oeste. An ancient Egyptian temple given by the Egyptian government to Spain when its original site was flooded by the construction of the Aswan Dam. Open Mon. to Sat. 10–1 and 5–8, Sun. and fiestas 10–3.

PARKS AND GARDENS. Jardin Botánico, to the south of the Prado, between Paseo del Prado and Retiro Park. First opened in 1781. Over 30,000 different species from all over the world. Open daily 10–8.

Casa del Campo, across the Manzanares from the Royal Palace. Formerly the royal hunting grounds, the land was first acquired by Philip II in 1599. Shady walks, lakeside cafe, rowing boats on the lake, sports center (with pool), jogging track, zoo and amusement park, among the attractions. To reach the park, take subway to El Lago or Batan, or bus 33 from Plaza de Isabel II, or—the best idea—cablecar from Paseo Rosales.

Parque del Oeste, on western edge of Madrid, off Paseo del Pintor Rosales. A pleasant park containing the Temple of Debod and a pretty rose garden.

Parque del Retiro. This shady, once-Royal, retreat *(retiro)* makes the perfect refuge from Madrid's relentless heat. Embellished with statues and fountains, and a beautiful rose garden, the park is at its liveliest Sunday mornings with buskers, puppet theaters, and much of Madrid out strolling. In summer there is an outdoor movie theater in La Chopera, and temporary exhibitions held in the Crystal Palace or the Palacio de Velázquez.

MUSIC, MOVIES AND THEATERS. Music. The main concert hall is the old *Opera,* or *Teatro Real* as it is also known, located opposite the Royal Palace, with its main entrance on Plaza Isabel II. Weekly concerts are given here, Oct. through Apr., by the Spanish National Orchestra and the National Radio and TV Orchestra, often under visiting conductors.

Other concerts are given in the *Teatro de la Zarzuela,* Jovellanos 4, in the auditorium of the *Fundación March* on Calle Castelló 77, and at the *Sala Fenix,* Paseo de la Castellana 37. A season of opera is held annually at the Teatro de la Zarzuela. Other concert venues include, sometimes, the *British Institute,* Almagro 5, the *French Institute* on Calle Marqués de Ensenada, and the *Washington Irving Center,* San Bernardo 107.

For program details, starting times and ticket prices, see the daily paper, *El País,* or the weekly leisure magazine, *Guía del Ocio,* available from newsstands all over Madrid.

Movies. Most foreign films shown in Spain are dubbed into Spanish, but there are about half a dozen cinemas in Madrid showing films in their original language with Spanish subtitles. Consult the local press, *El País* or *Guía del Ocio,* where these films will be marked "v.o." for *version original. El País* also lists cinemas showing subtitled films. A good cinema to try for films in English is the *Alphaville* (with four screens, entrance on Martín de los Heros) just off Plaza España. There is an official *Filmoteca* showing different films each day, always in their original language with Spanish subtitles. At presstime these showings were split between the *Círculo de Bellas Artes,* Marqués de Casa Riera 2 and the *Museo de Arte Contemporáneo,* Avda. Juan de Herrera in the University City. Most movie houses have three performances a day at roughly 4.30, 7.30 and 10.30. Tickets cost 250–350 ptas.

Theaters. If your Spanish is not very good, the legitimate theater is likely to be a complete loss to you. However, you won't need Spanish to enjoy a *zarzuela* or a musical revue. They're good fun. The best bet for non-Spanish-speaking visitors is the *Zarzuela,* Jovellanos 4, where you may see the top dance groups, operas, operetta and, of course, *zarzuela,* if it's the season. The *Teatro Español* at Príncipe 25, on Plaza Santa Ana, shows Spanish classics. The second of the state-sponsored theaters, usually showing plays of interest, is the *Teatro María Guerrero,* Calle Tamayo y Baus 4. The *Centro Cultural de la Villa de Madrid,* the underground theater on Plaza Colón, is an exciting contemporary theater.

Most theaters in Madrid have two curtains, at 7 and 10.30 P.M. They close one day during the week, usually Mon. Tickets are inexpensive and on the whole easy to obtain. With a few exceptions it is not at all unusual to buy tickets on the night of the performance. Details of plays are listed in *El País* and in *Guía del Ocio.*

SPORTS. Bullfighting comes first to mind, though most Spaniards would not wish to see it classified as a sport. Madrid has two main rings, so be careful you get the right one. If you have the opportunity during your stay, try to visit the big Ventas bullring, which seats 25,000. A smaller bullring is the Vista Alegre in the Carabanchel Bajo region across the Manzanares river. The bullfighting season in Madrid runs from April through October. There's almost always a fight Sundays, and often on Thursdays, too. Tickets can be bought in advance from Calle de la Victoria, off Carrera San Jerónimo, or at the bullring itself on the afternoon of the fight. The average Sunday *corridas* are now little more than a tourist spectacle—and not very good at that—but if you are intent on seeing a really good fight, try to be in Madrid around the middle of May during the San Isidro festivals; this will be your chance to witness some of the best fights in Spain, and tickets may well be hard to obtain.

Pelota is something you definitely shouldn't miss. It is the hardest, fastest ball game in the world. It is also a betting game, in which you get fast action for your money. If you want to try your luck, put 50 or 100 ptas. on Red or Blue and trust to luck. The handiest pelota court in Madrid is the Frontón Madrid, at Dr Cortezo 10. There is a session at 6 P.M. Mon.–Fri. and at 5.15 on Sat. Closed Sun.

Football (soccer) is now Spain's number one sport and has far surpassed bullfighting or pelota in popularity. It may be seen between September and May in the huge Santiago Bernabéu Stadium on the Castellana, home of Real Madrid, which holds 130,000 spectators, or in the Vicente Calderón Stadium, home of Madrid Atlético, near the Manzanares river. The final of the 1982 world cup was played in the Bernabéu Stadium on July 11. If you want to see **basketball** or even **baseball** (it's not unknown in Spain), check with your hotel porter on games that may be scheduled—depending of course, on the season. **Horse races** take place at the Hipodromo de la Zarzuela, on the Ctra de La Coruña, except in the summer months. **Car racing** at the Jarama Track, on the road to Burgos.

If you want exercise yourself, there is a fashionable and luxurious golf club, the Real Club de la Puerta de Hierro, on the Carretera de El Pardo. (Membership fees are prohibitively high, however.) Golf de Somosaguas, beside the Casa

MADRID

del Campo park, tel. 212 1647. Also Nuevo Club de Golf, at Las Matas at km. 26 on the Coruña highway, tel. 630 0820. For latter, membership not required, only a club card made out by your hotel. Club has pick-up service. There are plenty of places to **swim**—several of the 4- and 5-star hotels have pools, or you could try the Piscina El Lago, Avda. de Valladolid 37 or the Piscina Municipal, Avda. del Angel on Casa de Campo. You can play **tennis** also at the golf club, or at Casa del Campo, which has 15 all-weather courts.

Ice skating is at the Real Club in the Ciudad Deportiva, Paseo de la Castellana 175. There are two sessions daily, 11–1.45 and 5–11.45, and skates can be hired.

Greyhound racing is at the Canódromo Madrileño; buses leave from the Plaza Ramales. For **rowing,** there is the lake in the Retiro Park and the lake in the Casa de Campo, a much larger park across the Manzanares. In the winter, there is **skiing** in the sierra at Navacerrada. For **flying** enthusiasts, there exists the Royal Aero Club, with its airport at Cuatro Vientos; offices are at Carrera San Jerónimo 19.

SHOPPING. The large number of well-stocked stores sell everything imaginable. The glittering curio shops with their wares piled helter-skelter on dusty shelves, the richness and abundance of authentic works of art and, above all, the love and pride with which local goods are manufactured, make shopping in Madrid one of the chief attractions for anyone visiting this booming capital. Prices for most items are now on a par with those in England and the States.

Main Shopping Areas. Madrid has two main shopping areas. The first is in the center of town where the principal shopping streets are Gran Vía, the Calles de Preciados, del Carmen and Montera and Puerta del Sol. The second, and more elegant area—and naturally more expensive—is in the Salamanca district bounded by Serrano, Goya and Conde de Peñalver. There is another up-and-coming area in the north of town around Calle Orense and the Azca shopping center between Orense and the Castellana.

Department Stores. On the whole, visitors will generally find the best bargains in the department stores, in anything from souvenirs to furniture. Moreover, chances are you'll feel more at ease picking through the counters at your own speed than struggling to make yourself understood with the small shopkeepers. Virtually all department stores have interpreters available. The following is a list of the main stores.

Galerías Preciados is the longest-established department store in Madrid. Its main building is on Plaza Callao, right off the Gran Vía. Within the two seven-story buildings you'll find almost anything you may need. Another *Galerías* branch is located on Calle Arapiles near the Glorieta de Quevedo, and still another on Calle Goya, corner Conde de Peñalver. *Galerías Preciados* have now also taken over the old *Sear's* department store on Calle Serrano, corner of Ortega y Gasset. The Callao branch of *Galerías* is highly recommended for tourist souvenirs. Also outstanding are the Spanish ceramics, rugs, glassware and other handicrafts. Remains open throughout lunchtime.

El Corte Inglés in many ways is similar to *Galerías* and is its main competitor. There are four *Corte Ingléses* in Madrid: Calle Preciados, right near the Puerta del Sol; another one at the corner of Goya and Alcalá (also near the Goya *Galerías*); a third in the Urbanización Azca between the Castellana and Orense; and the fourth on the corner of Calle Princesa and Calle Alberto Aguilera. All have cafeterias. Quality of wares at the *Corte Inglés* is somewhat higher than that of *Galerías*. Best bet here, perhaps, are their leather goods. Remains open throughout lunchtime. The Preciados branch is probably the best.

Celso Garcia is a smaller, more intimate department store on Calle Serrano, corner of Ayala. Its goods tend to be of a higher quality and more exclusive taste. There is a huge new branch in the Azca shopping center on the Castellana.

Special Shopping Areas. One of the most interesting and colorful of the Madrid shopping areas is one you should save for a Sunday morning. It's the **Rastro** or Flea Market, which stretches down Ribera de Curtidores from El Cascorro statue, and extends over a maze of little side streets branching out from either side. Here, on a Sunday morning, you'll see an incredible display of secondhand odds and ends, spread out on blankets on the ground.

The central area, Curtidores, is more traditional. Here canvas booths have been set up to sell everything under the sun. Most of these, though, are cheap articles which are of little interest to the tourist, except for picture-taking.

If you want to try your hand at bargaining (which is a must here), there are booths selling everything conceivable. Buy with care, though, and don't carry money exposed. *Serious warning:* This place is an infamous hangout for pickpockets, who take advantage of the crowd's pushing and jostling. Women should leave pocketbooks behind and no one should take their passports or more money than they would mind losing.

From a buyer's viewpoint, the most interesting part of the Rastro is a series of galleries which line the street behind the booths. In dark shops built around picturesque patios, you can find all the antique dealers of Madrid represented. These shops, unlike the booths, are open all week during regular shopping hours, as well as on Sunday mornings. Here you can find old paintings and wood carvings, porcelain, furniture and jewelry. Also, in the *Nuevas Galerías,* Shop 45, you'll find a lapidary with unset precious, semi-precious and imitation gems which are well worth a look.

If you are a **stamp collector,** don't miss the *Stamp Fair,* held each Sunday and holiday morning from about 10 to 2 under the archways of Plaza Mayor.

Secondhand books can be bought all year round from the bookstalls on Cuesta Claudio Moyano, near Atocha railroad station. With a little browsing, you'll find curiosities and first editions. And if you're in Madrid at the end of May and the beginning of June, you can visit the National Book Fair, held in the Retiro Park from 10 A.M. to 10 P.M. daily. Here, Spanish booksellers offer both their newest releases and old standards—all at a 10% discount.

For **handicrafts** and **Toledo ware,** you will find literally hundreds of shops all over Madrid, many of which are reliable, some less so. Try the department stores first, particularly the *Corte Inglés* and *Galerías Preciados*. Then you might try *Artespaña,* the official Spanish government handicraft shop. They have branches at Gran Vía 32, Hermosilla 14 and Plaza de las Cortes 3. They have a wonderful assortment of all things Spanish—wood carvings, handwoven rugs, embroidered tablecloths, Majorcan glassware, attractive stone ornaments for gardens and rustic Spanish furniture. *Artespaña* will ship goods throughout the world and, being government-run, has reliable and reasonable prices.

Toledo wares are particularly good at *Artesanía Toledana,* Paseo del Prado, and at *El Escudo de Toledo,* next door on Plaza Cánovas del Castillo. In both these stores you'll find a large selection of daggers, swords, chess boards, paintings, fans, Lladró porcelain, guns and leather wine bottles. For **Granada wares,** marquetry, inlaid mother of pearl and so on, try *Artesanía Granadina,* Marqués de Casa Riera.

MADRID

Ceramics are a time-honored Spanish craft. Among the best examples are the exquisitely colored Manises lustrous glaze from Valencia, the blue and green designs from Granada, and the blue and yellow Talavera pottery and pretty greens from Puente del Arzobispo. They can be found in most of the large department stores where you can also find the famous Lladró porcelain. These delicate figures are made in the Lladró factory at Tabernes Blances just to the north of Valencia. Below are just one or two of the many shops you might try:

Original Hispana (O.H.1), Maestro Guerrero 1 behind the Hotel Plaza in Plaza de España. A vast and excellent display of Lladró.

AR, Gran Vía 46 on the corner of Calle Silva. Glass and porcelain including a good display of Lladró figures.

Cántaro, Flor Baja 8 just off Gran Vía, specializes in ceramics from all over Spain and ironwork.

The following areas are good for **antiques:** the Rastro, Calle del Prado, Carrera de San Jerónimo, Plaza de las Cortes, Plaza de Santa Ana.

For **fans,** try either the department stores or, for really superb examples, try the long-established *Casa de Diego* Puerta del Sol.

Shoes. A chapter apart are Spanish shoes for both men and women. You'll find them made of sturdy yet flexible leather, handcrafted in the latest styles and colors. The Spanish last is long and narrow so be very sure of trying your choice on carefully. Prices have gone up considerably, so unless shoes are very comfortable, don't buy them. Take a stroll along Gran Vía, San Jerónimo or Calle Serrano, where numerous shoe shops vie for attention.

Books. An excellent bookshop for maps and guidebooks is the *Librería Franco Española,* Gran Vía 54.

USEFUL ADDRESSES. Embassies. *American Embassy,* Serrano 75 (tel. 276 3600). *British Embassy,* Fernando el Santo 16 (tel. 419 1528/0208).

Police station. To report lost passports, stolen purses, etc., go to the police station at Calle de los Madrazos.

Main post office. Plaza de Cibeles.

Main telephone office. Red de San Luis on the Gran Vía.

Hospitals. The British–American Hospital is on Juan XXXIII no. 1 in the University City (tel. 234 6700).

Car hire. The most central offices of the main car-hire firms are: *Atesa,* Gran Vía 59 (tel. 248 9793); *Avis,* Gran Vía 60 (tel. 248 4203); *Europcar,* San Leonardo 8 (tel. 241 8892); *Hertz,* San Leonardo, corner of Maestro Guerrero just off Plaza de España (tel. 248 5803); *Ital,* Princesa 1 (tel. 241 2290). Central reservation numbers are *Atesa* (450 2062); *Avis* (457 9706); *Budget* (279 3400); *Europcar* (456 6013); *Hertz* (242 1000); *Ital* (402 1034).

Laundromats. *Lavomatic,* Bernardino López García 9. *Lavandería Maryland,* Meléndez Valdés 52. These are both self-service coin-operated launderettes. *Yulienka,* on Calle Conde Duque, will do your washing and ironing for you.

Left-luggage facilities. *Estación Sur de Autobuses,* Canarias 17, and at the air terminal beneath Plaza Colón.

Lost property. For items lost in city buses, Alcántara 26; in taxis, Alberto Aguilera 20; in the metro, the lost and found at Cuatro Caminos station.

American Express, Plaza de las Cortes 2 (tel. 222 1180). Open Mon. to Fri. 9–5.30 and Sat. 9–12.

Emergency phone numbers. Police 091; fire brigade 232 3232; ambulance 252 2792.

Airline offices. *Iberia* has several offices around the city, the main ones being at Velázquez 130 (tel. 261 9100), Princesa 2 (tel. 248 6683) and Plaza de

Cánovas del Castillo 5 (tel. 429 7443). The latter is perhaps the principal office and is the one you should go to if you are having problems with luggage lost on an Iberian flight. It is open Mon. to Fri. 9–7.30, Sat. 9–2. Ticket purchases on Sun. must be made at the airport. For 24-hour flight arrival and departure information, call *Inforiberia* on 411 2545. For reservations, call 411 2011 (30 lines) 8 A.M.–10 P.M.

British Airways is at Gran Vía 68 (tel. 205 4212/5076). Open Mon. to Fri. 9–6 only. The B.A. sales office at Barajas is open daily 9–7. *TWA* is at Gran Vía 68 (tel. 247 4200/248 0004). *Pan Am* is at Gran Vía 88 (tel. 241 4200/248 8535).

SPAIN AND THE SPANIARDS

A Changing Image

by
HARRY EYRES

Harry Eyres has lived, and traveled extensively, in Spain, both as a student and as the Spanish correspondent of the London Spectator, *for which he still writes on Spanish affairs.*

Spain—to risk one of the few generalizations that can be made about a land of such diversity—is the most individual country in Europe, and the Spanish are the most individualistic people. In fact, they are so individualistic that they find it difficult to accept the existence of anything as totalitarian as the Spanish nation. Spain has preserved its regional differences and identities better than other European nations, which gives it both the advantage of variety and the danger of disunity. It is a land of nationalisms rather than nationalism. The most violent, of course, is that of the Basques, with their strange prehistoric language and their terrorist independence movement, E.T.A. But the Basques are not the only Spaniards with their own language and pretensions to independence. Six million people on the east coast and in the Balearic islands speak Catalan, a language related to old Provencal, quite separate from Spanish, (which incidentally is known in Spain as Castilian), and equally rich in culture, history and tradition. Away in the wet northwest corner of the peninsula, the Galicians speak Gallego, which is related to Portuguese, and nurture their less vigorous dreams of an independent Galicia.

These complications should intrigue rather than disturb the visitor. Catalan street signs in Barcelona may be hard to decipher at first, but Catalans will speak Castilian if you ask them politely. Though E.T.A. have taken to planting bombs on beaches, they have so far confined their killing to the National Police and the Civil Guard.

Galloping Modernity

Indeed some visitors may prefer to forget altogether about political problems, relying on traditional images of bullfights and castanets, or beaches and sangría. Such things can be found, though the romantic idea of Spain is very much based on the South, and Andalusia in particular. Young Spaniards will not thank you for expecting them to conform to stereotypes of the torero or the haughty señorita. Among the more educated people there is a very strong wish to get away from all that paraphernalia, partly because it was promoted so strongly during the long repressive regime of Franco, whose belief in the immortal essence of Spain involved much artificial preservation of tradition. Most Spaniards now want to be modern and West European, not, as the Spanish Tourist Board used to say, "different."

There can be no denying that they have moved a very long way to that end in an extremely short space of time. What was still in the 1930s a rural and agricultural society has become predominantly urban and industrial, or even post-industrial. Ten years after the death of Europe's second last surviving Fascist dictator, Spain has a democratic system headed by a sane and tactful constitutional monarch, and a socialist government—voted in by an enormous majority—for the first time since the short-lived Second Republic of 1931–36.

That earlier period of democracy ended in the carnage of the Civil War, which seemed for a long time (its memory was fostered by Franco) to have reaffirmed the Black Legend of Spain's tragic destiny. Spaniards now do not like to talk about it, but more out of a wish to forget a time of appalling waste than because of unhealed wounds. When Lt. Col. Tejero of the Guardia Civil walked into the Cortes (Parliament) brandishing a pistol on 23 February 1981, it appeared for a short time as if Spain's renascent democracy had been ended once again by a military coup. When this attempt failed, however, almost entirely because of King Juan Carlos's firm and immediate appeal to the army to remain loyal to him as its commander-in-chief, it proved instead that the new democracy in Spain had been strengthened by its first serious ordeal. Future threats from the Armed Forces, the only real danger to the democratic system, had become suddenly less credible.

The final confirmation, for most Spaniards, that their country has shrugged off its persistent image of backwardness, is Spain's acceptance into the European club, the E.E.C. What benefits this will bring remain to be seen—and there are some who even dare to doubt that it *will* bring substantial benefits—but its psychological importance cannot be doubted. Fernando Morán, then Spanish Foreign Minister, summed it up when he said after terms had been agreed in March 1985: "now at last Spain can hold her head high once more in international relations."

Perhaps even more important than this political modernization is the drastic liberalization which has occurred in Spanish society. From being one of the most conservative countries in Western Europe, Spain has suddenly become, in certain respects, one of the most liberal. The taking of some soft drugs, for example, is now permitted, even if their sale is not (though the vendors of so-called "chocolate" at the entrance to the arcaded Plaça Reial in Barcelona do not seem to be aware of this). It must be said that many people are linking the rise in crime on the streets with the availability of drugs, and there are signs of the government backpedalling on this issue. Abortion is now legal, though only for medical reasons or after rape—and here too there are signs of a conservative backlash, because the Constitutional Court recently (1985) ruled against the Socialist government's pro-abortion legislation —though only on a technicality. Pornography, banned for so long under the "muy católico" Generalissimo Franco, is back on the streets, and it seems to be making up for lost time. Pornographic comics, strangely combining strip (in both senses) cartoons with radical politics are popular with the student generation, who have been going through all the styles, fashions and movements which Spain missed out on from the '50s to the '80s, rock'n'roll to punk, in an accelerated rampage. Toplessness is rife on the crowded beaches, despite the disapproval of the Catholic organization Opus Dei and the right-wing daily paper *A.B.C.*

The Spanish Landscape

Despite all this evidence of Spain's modernity, however, it may still be that it is the anachronistic and, dare one say, "different" elements of the country which will interest and attract the visitor most. Under this heading come history, culture and many aspects of the way of life in Spain which still contrast (and we at least may be grateful for it) with the increasingly homogenized world outside. One thing not much affected by modernization is the landscape, or at least its more permanent features, the mountains, the light, the sea—if we forget for the moment the ghastly ribbon development which has spoilt so much of what Rose Macaulay in the 1950s could still call its "fabled shore."

Spain is a large country by European standards, only slightly smaller than France, twice the size of Britain, and it contains an extraordinary variety of geography and, above all, climate, which goes far towards explaining the strength of regional character and identity noted earlier. It might be better to think of Spain as a subcontinent than a country. Certainly the idea of a uniformly "sunny Spain" is misleading, but not as misleading as the English ditty "The rain in Spain falls mainly on the plain," which, if you take the plain to mean the central tableland or meseta, is precisely the opposite of the truth. This plateau (about 2,000 feet high) which covers two-fifths of the peninsula is parchingly arid for most of the year, as are large stretches of the eastern coastal region and the southwestern region of Extremadura. The northwestern "nationality" of Galicia, on the other hand, is wetter than Ireland, with which it has much in common. This excess of humidity is very much the exception in Spain, and it is a costly irony of fate that rainfall should be highest in areas where the soil is poorest. Aridity is the keynote, and nowhere is this brought home more vividly than at the historic pass of Roncesvalles, where Roland made his last stand, which connects the French *département des Pyrenées Occidentales* with the little Spanish kingdom of Navarre. In summer, looking from the Spanish side, you see a bank of cloud like smoke rolling through the defile from the damp deciduous forests of beech and chestnut which cover the French western Pyrenees, then dissolving into blue sky as it reaches the great golden-tawny expanse of the Navarrese plain.

Such a color can only be produced by long hours of burning sun. The summer sun in Spain is often more awesome than, as the tourist brochures stupidly reiterate, pleasant and sexy. It is capable of obliterating all activity and reducing one to utter torpor. Unlike that of northern countries, Spanish sun can have a negative or destructive value. It ages people prematurely and etches bitter lines in those faces which we picturesquely associate with Picasso peasants. On the other hand, it relaxes the muscles and dissolves away many of the neuroses which afflict people from sunless lands. A Spanish Edvard Munch is inconceivable. In winter, spring and autumn the extra light and heat which the northerner will experience can only be a bonus. I have breakfasted outside under the lemon tree on my patio in Barcelona on Christmas Eve with the thermometer standing at 70°, and throughout November and December there will be days, in the low-lying areas at least, when it is as warm as high summer in England. Even in January and February, when the temperature often falls below zero in Madrid, the weather is frequently bright and cloudless, and the crystalline light of Castile exhilarating, however cold the air.

Apart from the sun-baked dryness, the most striking feature of the Spanish landscape is its ruggedness. This is, after Switzerland, the second most mountainous country in Europe, containing its highest roads and villages. This means ample opportunities for skiing in ranges like the Pyrenees, the Sierra Nevada, the Guadarrama and the Picos de Europa. It also means innumerable remote and lovely valleys, often deserted by nearly all their former inhabitants in the drift towards the towns, where those who favor adventurous holidays can hunt, fish, walk, or just find an almost overwhelming peace camping in the open or sleeping in derelict farmhouses. Such relics of paradise exist, for example, three hours drive from Barcelona in the Catalan hinterland, where you can find yourself quite literally in another world. The experience can be disorientating, but will not be easily forgotten.

Early History

To some people this romantic notion of getting away from it all and communing with nature will seem nostalgic, unrealistic, or simply boring. Human activity, which in its more memorable forms means culture and history, will be the focus of their attention. Spanish culture and history have of course been decisively influenced by geography. The three features of that geography to note here are the barrier of the Pyrenees, neatly isolating Spain from the rest of Europe, the proximity to Africa (indeed W.H. Auden described Spain as "that fragment nipped off from hot Africa soldered so crudely to inventive Europe"), and the outlook westwards to the Americas.

Not that the Pyrenees have ever been an impassable barrier—first the Carthaginians, to attack the Romans, then the Romans, to defeat the Carthaginians, found it possible to cross them repeatedly. In the end Spain, or rather two Spains, Hispania Citerior and Hispania Ulterior (and the plurality may be significant) became part of the Roman empire: they produced four emperors as well as literary figures as distinguished as the Senecas, Martial and Lucan. The most important evidence of Roman dominion is the language, or languages (again plural)—Castilian, Catalan and Gallego, but not of course Basque, are all members of the Romance family—but there are also imposing physical remains like the aqueduct at Segovia and the theater and other ruins in the Extremaduran city of Mérida. No question then that Spain was very much part of Western Europe.

The Moorish Inheritance

It did not stay that way. In 711 the troubled period of Visigothic rule ended when Spain was invaded by Arabs from North Africa, who overran the country in an astonishingly short space of time. The Moorish rule which prevailed throughout much of the peninsula for the next seven-and-a-half centuries was generally tolerant—far more tolerant, most historians consider, than the Christian rule which followed—and it produced peaks of civilization which Spain has since rarely, if ever, surpassed.

The influence of the Moors on Spain is a huge subject which can only be touched on here. It is certainly not confined to the 4,000 odd Arabic words (including nearly all those beginning "al," like "alcalde," "alcázar," "albañil" and so on), or the beautiful remains of Moorish architecture, but persists in ethnic and, more interestingly, social characteristics which are the legacy of those 750 years of intermingling. Still, the architecture is what most tourists will want to see. It is difficult to say anything new about the Alhambra at Granada, but it *is* delicate and superbly civilized and one of the few wonders of the world in which you could want to live. Personally I prefer the Generalife, with its famous gardens but also less restored and therefore more evocative buildings. Manuel de Falla's *Nights in the Gardens of Spain* (one of the few great pieces of Spanish music not written by a Frenchman) is a wonderful recreation of its atmosphere of delicate and sensual beauty.

The most amazing Moorish building in Spain is not of course in Granada, but in Córdoba: the grand mosque or Mezquita, whose vast interior supported by over 800 columns, as Richard Ford rightly and simply said in the first handbook to Spain, "cannot be described, it must be seen." Hidden away in this forest or labyrinth of striped marble is a fair-sized Christian cathedral. It was ordered to be built by the

Emperor Charles V, who also knocked down part of the Alhambra to construct a Renaissance palace, vilified by most guide writers, but to me a telling contrast to its surroundings. Charles however was not pleased when he saw how his orders had been carried out in Córdoba, and he rebuked the clerical authorities in resonant words which convey his generous appreciation of the culture he was annihilating: "You have built here what you, or anyone, might have built anywhere else; but you have destroyed what was unique in the world."

He and his successors did not take this message to heart. Andalusia has never recovered the prosperity it enjoyed at the height of Moorish rule.

The Conquest of the Americas

Having rooted out the cultured Moors and the rich and industrious Jews from their own land, the Catholic Kings turned their attention overseas. The colonization of Central, South and parts of North America was an astonishing feat, carried out, like the unification of Spain itself, in just one generation. Whether it had an altogether positive value, either for the colonies or for Spain itself, is debatable: in our post-colonial, post-imperial age the destruction of the Aztec, Maya and Inca cultures is likely to seem more shameful than heroic, especially when the Spanish administrations which replaced them have become the byword for seediness and corruption. However, Hispano-America still exists, and forms a kind of cultural commonwealth with Spain of which Spaniards at least feel proud, and is now showing signs of sloughing off its centuries-old apathy and emerging into the modern world. Its literary culture, revived by such figures as Borges, García Márquez and Vargas Llosa, is at the moment second to none.

For Spain herself, the colonization of the Americas was both her greatest achievement and the cause of her long decline. Instead of stimulating the economy, Peruvian gold and Bolivian silver encouraged indolence and produced inflation. At the same time religious dogmatism and at times fanaticism (the Inquisition is not entirely a legend) gave rise to costly religious wars, and then isolation from Protestant Europe. The first centralized state in Europe put unity above everything else, and kept itself together, just, at the cost of the prosperity which the rising capitalist system was bringing to other parts of Europe. The naturally bourgeois, trading, capitalist Catalans resented this, tried to break away, and were crushed in two bloody wars which have not been forgotten to this day. The Catalans' heyday had been in the 13th, 14th and 15th centuries when their mercantile empire extended as far as Athens and they produced literature, art and architecture to match any in Europe. The *barrio gótico* (including the cathedral with its idyllic cloister full of trees and geese) and the church of Santa Maria del Mar in Barcelona, as well as the majestic cathedrals of Palma and Gerona, still bear ample witness to the glories of Catalan Gothic.

SPAIN AND THE SPANIARDS 59

Art and Culture

From the late 16th century onwards, Spain, ruled by introverted monarchs like Philip II, turned in on herself. Her architecture, after the rich Plateresque period when stone was treated like gold or silver, acquired a somber austerity, epitomized by Philip's grey granite monastery, which looks more like a Ministry, the Escorial. In painting, as well as fine devotional artists of widely different character like the ascetic Zurbarán and the gentle Murillo, Spain in the 17th century produced the first of her indigenous, isolated universal geniuses in Velázquez. The Velázquez rooms in the Prado are a must for anyone interested not just in Spain but in European culture, and in themselves make a nonsense of Kenneth Clark's omission of Spain from his personal view of civilization.

The next great Spanish pictorial genius was Goya, and it would not be much of an exaggeration to say that he was the next thing of any real interest to happen in Spain after Velazquez's death in 1660. Once again the Prado is the place to appreciate the full range of this extraordinary artist who managed to combine vitality and grace with horror and despair.

Goya ended his days in Bordeaux, and exile or emigration became a familiar fate of Spanish artists and intellectuals from his day until very recent times. The rest of the 19th century was not a happy time for Spain (though it produced two great novelists in Pérez Galdós and Leopoldo Alas), and the century ended, symbolically, with the loss of her remaining colonies in the disastrous wars of 1898. In fact, the annus terribilis of 1898 became a symbol not just of military defeat but also of intellectual regeneration. Chastened by the events of that year, which seemed to indicate a near-terminal decline from the days of national greatness, a group of writers, of whom Unamuno and Ortega y Gasset are the most famous, set about examining the state of the nation's soul.

The first three decades of this century were altogether an astonishingly vital creative period in Spain. Apart from the poets there were the painters Picasso, Gris and the Catalans Miró and Dalí, and Dalí's friend and Surrealist collaborator the film director Luis Buñuel. Picasso and Miró have their own museums, both beautifully housed, in Barcelona, and Dalí has his idiosyncratic one in his native town of Figueras. These men were experimenters at the forefront of the avant-garde impetus of European art at that time, which went so far beyond the present that looking at it now one feels passé. Equally modern, but in a different, highly religious spirit, is the work of the Catalan architect Antoni Gaudí. His church of the Holy Family (Sagrada Familia) in Barcelona, which looks like a cross between a Gothic cathedral and a flight of rockets, is still not finished, and will not be for a century or two, but it is still one of the world's most impressive buildings. How tragic then that all this creative exuberance, fostered by the relatively benign dictatorship of Primo de Rivera in the 1920s, then the Republic of the 1930s, was dissipated by the Civil War. It is only now, after 40 years of stifling repression under Franco, that culture can breathe again in Spain. Some exciting work is certainly being done—filmmakers like

Victor Erice and Carlos Saura have at last provided a worthy succession to Buñuel—and Madrid now considers itself to be the cultural capital of Europe.

The Art of Living

There is a sense in which all this talk of culture and history is beside the point—the point being that Spain's special strength has always been in popular culture rather than high culture, the art of living rather than fine art. Spain's ultimate art-form is the fiesta, a popular religious celebration which turns into a street party, and embraces dance, processions, masquerade and bullfight. The fiesta is not a piece of phoney folklore artificially preserved for tourists, but an integral part of Spanish life. Fiesta is also the ordinary Spanish word for party. The biggest one of all takes place every July in Pamplona—ten solid days of drinking, dancing, bull-running and bullfighting, called the Sanfermines after the town's patron saint (who may never have existed). The whole affair, despite the religious processions, is profoundly pagan and bacchanalian. Many tourists take part in it, but they are easily absorbed into the mass of Spaniards who come from all parts of the peninsula, thieves and beggars as well as aficionados, swelling the population of Pamplona to twice its normal size of 150,000. It is a joyful, liberating and totally exhausting experience (not to go to bed, at night anyway, for the duration of the fiesta is a point of honor), and the real heroes are the waiters who maintain an incredibly professional 24-hour service against all odds. The would-be heroes are those who run with the bulls every morning through the narrow Calle Estafeta to the bullring armed only with a rolled-up newspaper. As several people get gored every year, and fatalities are not uncommon, this is a sport best left to the local lads, who know what they are doing. As for the bullfights themselves, by all means go to one, with Hemingway at your side (though you will find queueing for seats in Pamplona a frustrating exercise), for they are a genuine and unique part of Spanish popular culture, but if you are like me you will find them not so much revolting as ultimately boring.

Every night of the Sanfermines a band plays in the Plaza del Castillo until four A.M., and the locals, dressed in white with red sashes, dance with a grace which makes the foreigner feel ashamed and envious. All Spanish people seem able to dance well, no matter what age they are, and every part of the country has preserved its indigenous traditional dances. These range from the statuesque Sardana of Catalonia, with its strong nationalistic overtones, to the passionate, very unEuropean flamenco of Andalusia.

Eating Well

I described the waiters as the heroes of the Sanfermines, and waiters are perhaps the most important professional group in Spain. The enormous success of tourism in Spain must be largely owing to them, and the fact that there is no other country in Europe at least where one can eat and drink in so civilized a manner at so modest a cost. The sheer

SPAIN AND THE SPANIARDS

number of bars and restaurants is staggering, but even more important is the flexibility they offer in terms of one's being able to eat or drink anything one wants from eight in the morning until two the next, and above all the ease of atmosphere which makes eating and drinking out seem the most natural thing in the world.

As for the food and drink themselves, I have never understood why Spanish cuisine has such a dubious reputation. The abundance of good ingredients, fresh fish (available everywhere), olive oil, tomatoes, cheese from La Mancha, and the very limited encroachment of fast food, make eating a constant pleasure even at a simple level. In the smart restaurants of Madrid and Barcelona, you can enjoy genuine haute cuisine at a fraction of what it costs in France. Spanish wine, even if it cannot reach the heights of the finest from France and Germany, offers the best value in Europe. I lived happily for months on a mellow Valdepeñas which cost 70 pesetas a bottle; excellent Riojas and Penedes wines can be had for only three or four times that amount, as can sherry and delicious bubbly (now that Spain is in the E.E.C. it can no longer be called champagne) from San Sadurní de Noia. Brandy is perhaps too cheap, and if it wants to tackle the problem of alcoholism, the Spanish government should consider raising the duty on hard liquor, which until recently stood at 1 peseta a bottle.

I have left until last what I consider the best thing Spain can offer, and that is an evening spent going round bars or "tascas" eating tapas. Tapas are small dishes, usually eaten to the accompaniment of equally small glasses of wine or sherry, and they consist of things like fried fish or shellfish (any number of different varieties), slices of cured ham, olives and devilled eggs. Each bar in tapa centers like the Calle Echegaray in Madrid, the Parte Vieja of San Sebastián or the Calle de la Merced in Barcelona has its own specialty. I would like to leave you in one of those places, where you will encounter a heartwarming openness and hospitality, as you get to know the generous people of Spain, and conclude for yourself whether their country is different and romantic, or modern and European, or just, as they will often tell you, a disaster. Few visitors will agree with that: most will want to return.

SPAIN'S HISTORY AND ART

Land of Contrast

by
AILSA HUDSON

Spain, the crossroads between Africa and Europe, the Atlantic and the Mediterranean, is a country of striking contrasts. On the one hand, this gigantic peninsula offers a welcoming coastline of natural harbors and fertile foreshores, but on the other, for those who penetrate it more deeply, it throws up barriers of high sierras and plateaux, with a rude climate and sparse resources. The coastal fringe seems to turn its back on the central mesetas, and mirrors the history of Spain—a ceaseless struggle between the will to unite and the tendency to dispersion and isolation, still seen today in the struggle of the Catalans and the Basque separatists.

The history you see in the coastal Greek and Roman remains at Ampurias, the Moorish palaces and mosques of Granada and Toledo in the south, and the splendid royal residences of the interior, has been largely determined by the diverse physical background of the country.

To grasp some understanding of the peoples and culture which greet you today, it is essential to know something of the colorful and often turbulent past which has shaped them.

SPAIN'S HISTORY AND ART

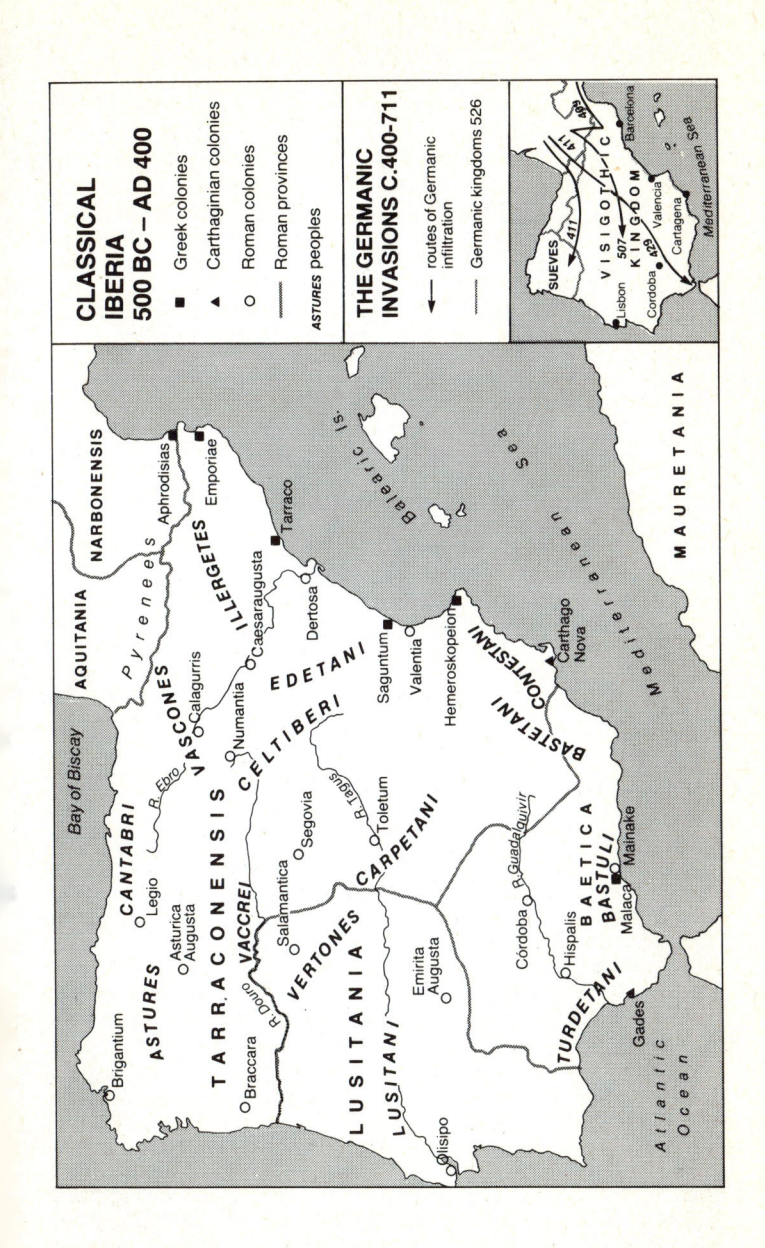

CLASSICAL IBERIA 500 BC – AD 400

- ■ Greek colonies
- ▲ Carthaginian colonies
- ○ Roman colonies
- — Roman provinces
- ASTURES peoples

THE GERMANIC INVASIONS C.400-711

- → routes of Germanic infiltration
- — Germanic kingdoms 526

From the Phoenicians to the Visigoths

c. 1100 B.C.	Earliest Phoenician colonies, including Cádiz, Villaricos, Almuñécar and Málaga
c. 650	Beginning of Greek colonization of the eastern seaboard
237–206	*Carthage v. Rome*—237 Carthaginians land in Spain; c. 225 Cartagena founded by Hasdrubal as capital of the Carthaginian colony; 219 Hannibal's successful siege of Sagunto, a Roman ally, precipitates the Second Punic War; 218 The Romans under Scipio Calvus land at Ampurias to assault Carthaginian supply lines in Spain; 212 Romans capture Sagunto; 209 Scipio Africanus captures Cartagena and uses it as his base for the defeat of the Carthaginians in Spain; 206 Carthaginians expelled from Spain
138	Roman conquest of Galicia
121	Roman conquest of the Balearic Islands
29–19	The Cantabrian War brings the whole of Spain under Roman domination
A.D. 67	St. Paul is said to have visited Spain
74	The Edict of Vespasian extends rights of Roman citizenship to all Spaniards
200s	Christian communities established throughout Spain
380	Emperor Theodosius I, a Spaniard, proclaims Christianity the only tolerated religion throughout the empire
409	The first wave of Germanic invaders, the Sueves and the Vandals, reach Spain, signalling the end of the period of classical culture. Settling in Iberia by treaty with Rome, they set up a series of kingdoms broadly based on the old Roman colonies

The settlement of Spain dates from an early age. Paleolithic remains have been found in abundance at many sites, including the famous caves at Altamira painted with animals and hunting scenes, the "Sistine Chapel of Prehistoric art." During the second millennium B.C. the northern, western and southern parts of the Iberian peninsula shared a copper age culture with much of northwest Europe, characterized by megalithic structures, passage graves and extensive mineral exploitation. Mineral wealth led to Spain's early emergence as a trading and exporting centre, and during the first millennium B.C. it attracted Phoenician, Greek and eventually Carthaginian traders and settlers. The remains of their towns and cities still scatter the eastern seaboard.

By this time the native inhabitants can be broadly divided into the Iberians in the south, the Basques in the western Pyrenees, and the Celts who had colonized much of northern Iberia.

The influence of the Mediterranean colonists upon the native peoples was limited to the coastal zones, but some fine examples exist of hybrid sculpture, such as the *Lady of Elche* (Archeological Museum, Madrid).

Carthaginian aggression finally provided their rivals, the Romans, with a pretext for resuming open warfare. During the Second Punic War (219–202 B.C.), despite Hannibal's successes in Italy, Rome thrust out at Spain. By the end of the war Carthaginian forces had been totally expelled from Spain, and Rome with its usual ruthless efficiency proceeded to conquer the interior and the west.

SPAIN'S HISTORY AND ART

The coastal regions of Spain were quickly Romanized, but resistance elsewhere was fierce and the invasion took over 75 years to complete. The Romans brought with them their institutions, their language, law and order, tailor-made local government, roads and, in later years, Roman citizenship and Christianity, all of which left an indelible mark. They rapidly exploited Spain's natural resources, lead, silver, iron ore, tin and gold being mined unceasingly during the first two centuries A.D. Andalusia became Rome's granary, and wine, olive oil and horses were other major exports. The peninsula soon became the pre-eminent colony outside Italy, and indeed a number of outstanding Roman figures were born in Spain, including the emperors Trajan and Hadrian, and the writers Seneca, Martial and Quintilian.

The extent and permanence of Roman colonization is demonstrated by the wealth of remains which are still visible throughout Spain today. These include many towns and cities, such as Tarragona, Sagunto (near Valencia), Itálica (near Seville) and Mérida (near Badajoz), and remarkable civil engineering feats, such as the 128-arch aqueduct at Segovia and the bridge at Alcántara. Ampurias has Greek and Roman remains side by side.

The beginning of the fifth century A.D. brought the gradual decline of Roman dominance in Spain, as the infiltration of Germanic peoples which had occurred elsewhere in the empire finally reached the Iberian peninsula. The Sueves, Alans and Vandals crossed the Pyrenees in 409 and within two years had established themselves in separate kingdoms, ending the endurance and continuity of the classical era.

Christians and Muslims

419	Visigoths establish themselves in northern Spain, creating a large kingdom with its capital at Toulouse
507	Toledo becomes Visigothic capital
558	Extension of Visigothic rule to include much of the south, and the kingdom of the Sueves in the west
587	Visigothic king Reccared embraces Catholicism: enforced baptism of Jews follows
711	Invasion from North Africa by Muslim Berber armies. King Roderick defeated and Visigothic kingdom destroyed
712	Muslim invasion completed, Visigothic resistance isolated in a strip of Christian states across the north of Spain. Muslim capital established at Córdoba, and the territory administered as an emirate of the Ummayad Caliphate of Damascus
718	Pelayo, successor of Roderick, creates the kingdom of Asturias; the Christian reconquest of Spain is launched
732	Muslim expansion north of the Pyrenees halted by the Franks at Poitiers; Muslims withdraw to Iberia
756	Abd al-Rahman I establishes semi-independent Ummayad dynasty in Spain
777	Frankish invasion of Spain under Charlemagne checked at Zaragoza
778	Charlemagne's retreat shattered at Roncesvalles, but Franks establish rule over Spain north of the Ebro
837	Muslim suppression of Christian and Jewish revolts
899	Miraculous discovery of remains of St. James the Greater, foundation of the church of Santiago de Compostela

912–961	Reign of Abd al-Rahman III, the apogee of Ummayad culture. Reorganization of government, navy, agriculture and industry
c.930–970	Rise of Count Fernán González of Burgos, establishing Castile as autonomous Christian power
970–1035	Sancho the Great unites Castile and Navarre and begins the conquest of León
976–1009	Reign of Hisham II, effectively deposed by Hajib al-Mansur whose brilliant administrative reforms and successful campaigns against the Christian kingdoms briefly revives flagging Ummayad power
1002	Death of al-Mansur, followed by power struggles, civil war and the disintegration of centralized Ummayad authority

Despite the barbarian name-tag, the peoples who settled in the northern and western regions of the later Roman empire saw themselves for the most part as successors to and preservers of Roman culture and the resident Hispano-Romans (who out-numbered the Visigoths five to one) continued to exist much as before. Prior to the baptism of Reccared and the reforms of Receswinth, the Visigoths maintained their own religion and civil code, but with the extension of their territory throughout the peninsula a centralized system of law, religion and government became necessary. Something of the classical heritage was revived and preserved, reflected in the encyclopedic works of Isidore of Seville, and in the Visigothic architectural decoration in Córdoba cathedral and the church of San Juan de Baños de Cerrato, near Palencia, built by Receswinth.

However, the economic and strategic importance of Spain encouraged attempts at invasion by the Franks and the Byzantines. The third such attempt, by the Islamic Berbers, was successful. Within seven years Iberia was conquered, and Christian resistance limited to pockets in the north. Islamic expansion was finally checked by Charlemagne, but with the Ummayad dynasty in firm control of Spain south of the Ebro a period of cultural blossoming began. In many ways the Arabs were the heirs to classical culture. They were largely tolerant of Christians and Jews living in their realm. They embellished and improved much of the legacy of Roman civilization, introducing new plants and agricultural techniques, reinvigorating manufacturing and trade and introducing distinctive styles and motifs still traceable in modern ceramics, carpets and folk music. They built palaces, mosques, libraries and schools; many of those buildings which survive in Andalusia were built much later, but the 850 columns elaborating the mosque at Córdoba and the smaller mosque at Toledo testify to the magnificence of early Moorish architecture. The distinctive characteristics of this style are the horseshoe arches and extensive geometric and floral patterns intermingled with Kufic script.

The polyglot nature of Moorish society permitted the fertile intermingling of many groups and factions—there was exchange and respect between the localised groups of each faith, as well as intermittent revolts and power struggles. It was against this backdrop, in the first half of the eighth century, that a substantial Christian state developed in Asturias. The moral strength of the Christian north was boosted

SPAIN'S HISTORY AND ART

considerably by the apparent discovery of the remains of St. James the Greater, and the foundation of the cathedral of Santiago de Compostela, which has remained an important pilgrimage centre. By the tenth century, mainly under the leadership of Castile, the Christian states rallied sufficiently to begin the long task of reconquest.

The Reconquest

1065–1109 *Reign of Alfonso VI of Castile* who led the revival of the Christian reconquest of Spain; 1085 Toledo captured by Alfonso VI; 1086 The Almoravids enter Spain to help combat the Christians. Alfonso VI defeated at Zallaka; c.1091 Muslim Spain integrated with the Almoravid empire; 1087–88 Rodrigo Díaz de Bivar, known as El Cid (Lord), re-enters the service of Alfonso VI. A knight of Burgos (in whose cathedral he and his wife are buried), he served under Sancho II of Castile. Exiled in 1081 he returned to help the Christian assault, but subsequently served the Muslim ruler of Zaragoza. He eventually ruled Valencia. After his death (1099) Valencia was regained by the Almoravids

1126–57 *Alfonso VII of Castile* takes the Christian offensive; 1137 Aragón unites with Catalonia, forming a new Christian power centered on Zaragoza; 1144 Christian attacks on Andalusia; 1146 The Almohades come to the defence of Moorish Spain, eventually taking complete control

1158–1214 *Reign of Alfonso VIII of Castile* who leads a series of successful campaigns against the Moors; 1195 Alfonso VIII defeated by the Moors at Alarcos, but, supported by Pope Innocent III he prepares for a major assault; 1212 Victory at Las Navas de Tolosa by united Christian armies. Almohades expelled from Spain and Moorish power limited to the kingdom of Granada; 1214 Catalonia secured from the Franks by the Aragonese at Muret

1213–76 Reign of Jaime I the Conqueror of Aragón who regained the Balearics (1229–35), Valencia (1238) and Murcia, which he ceded to Castile

1230–52 Reign of Ferdinand III (St. Ferdinand) of Castile and León, who conquered Córdoba (1236) and Seville (1248)

1252–84 Reign of Alfonso X the Wise of Castile, scholar, astronomer, poet, historian and codifier of the law

1270 End of the main period of the Reconquest, as Portugal concentrates on control of the Atlantic coast, Aragón seeks power in the Mediterranean, and Castile enters a period of dynastic power struggles

Although this period saw the gradual decline of Moorish power and the establishment of three increasingly distinct and secure Christian states in Portugal, Castile and Aragón, the Christian states remained almost continually under arms, while the Muslims saw the establishment of two powerful dynasties, the Almoravids and Almohades, both marked by considerable cultural achievements. The Alcázar and the Giralda still dominate Seville today and, with the Alhambra at Granada (completed in the 14th century), are unique in Islamic architecture, a true fusion of Moorish and local styles.

SPAIN'S HISTORY AND ART

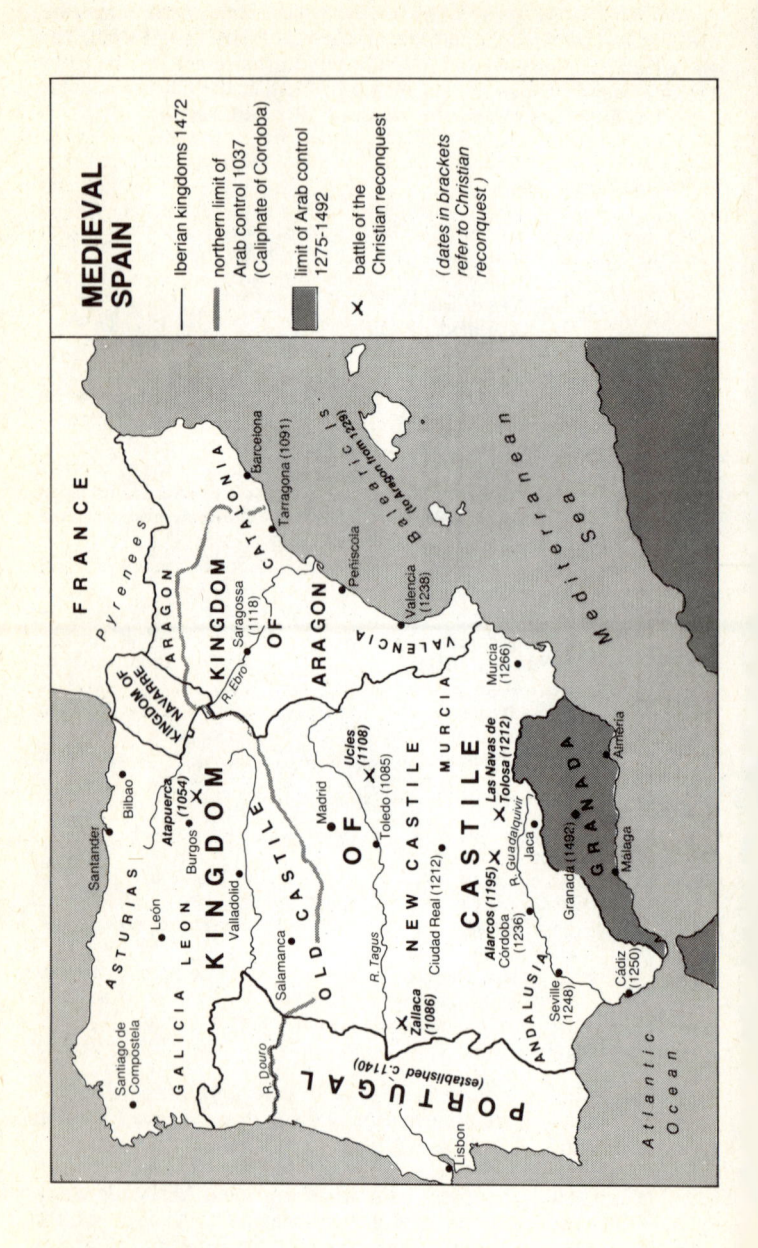

MEDIEVAL SPAIN

— Iberian kingdoms 1472
— northern limit of Arab control 1037 (Caliphate of Cordoba)
▨ limit of Arab control 1275-1492
✗ battle of the Christian reconquest

(dates in brackets refer to Christian reconquest)

SPAIN'S HISTORY AND ART

Arabic scholasticism continued to advance, with the first major universities being founded at Valencia (1209) and Salamanca (1242). The work of outstanding Arabic scholars provided a direct link with the classical past long after the Reconquest was complete. Idrisi the geographer and the philosopher Averroes were both active in the 12th century, as were Mainonides who translated medical texts and Sarasorda who introduced Muslim mathematics to the West. One aspect of the intermingling of Islamic and Christian cultures was the development of lyrical poetry and the art of the troubadour. The exploits of El Cid were a popular subject and probably first recorded in the 12th century in the *Cantar de Mio Cid*.

Throughout the period the strength of the Church remained stable. Carolingian and then Romanesque architecture, derived from southern French models, was developed most spectacularly at Santiago de Compostela. Later, the High Gothic style made its appearance in the building of the cathedrals of Toledo (c.1230), Burgos (1126) and León (c.1230). Catalan Gothic can be seen in the cathedrals of Barcelona (1298) and Gerona (1312).

The Reconquest also had a lasting effect on the social structure of Spain. The Christian kingdoms developed a nobility based on military achievement and as the Reconquest proceeded south such figures were granted substantial domains—some still owned by their descendants. At a slightly lower level were the wealthy knights—*infanzones* and *hidalgos*—a class which was created by and lived for force of arms. It was this chivalric brotherhood which carried Spanish might overseas to Holland, the Americas and the Indies after the Reconquest—but which also provided the model for Don Quixote.

However, the gradual process of Reconquest also held back the development of feudalism, and the long tradition of guerrilla warfare in Castile led to a concentration of the population in towns, and an impoverishment of agriculture which still exists today.

Minority groups, including Jews and non-belligerent Muslims, continued to live unhampered in the Christian states. The piecemeal granting of communal sovereignty still influences local politics, and forms the spine of the arguments for separatism voiced today.

The High Middle Ages

1282	Peter (Pedro) III adds Sicily to the Aragonese kingdom; Aragón becomes the principle power in the western Mediterranean
1295	Frederick I of Sicily establishes dynasty independent of Aragón
1340	Alfonso XI of Castile ends the threat of the Moroccan Muslims at Rio Salado
1374	Peace of Almazan between Castile, and Portugal and Aragón
1409	Martin of Aragón reunites Aragón and Sicily, ending a period of dynastic struggle
1435	Alfonso V of Aragón and Sicily conquers Naples and southern Italy, transferring the center of power away from the Spanish mainland to Italy
1454–74	Reign of Henry IV of Castile, during which the rivalry and anarchic power of the nobility reaches its height
1469	Marriage of Isabella, princess of Castile, to Ferdinand, heir to the

	throne of Aragón; this marriage becomes the key to Spanish unity
1474	Isabella succeeds to the Castilian throne
1478	Establishment of the Inquisition
1479	Ferdinand succeeds to the throne of Aragón, Catalonia and Valencia. The rule of the combined Catholic crowns restores royal power in Castile
1492	Conquest of the last Moorish outpost of Granada makes Ferdinand and Isabella rulers of all Spain. Attempted conversion of Muslims and Jews follows; subsequent expulsion of all Jews; first voyage of Christopher Columbus, under the patronage of Isabella, discovers the West Indies. Further voyages (1493, 1498 and 1502) establish the existence of the Americas
1494	Treaty of Tordesillas whereby Portugal and Spain divide the non-European world into two spheres of influence. Almost all of the known Americas and the Philippines fell under Spanish rule in the 16th century
1502	Uprising of Moors in Castile leads to forcible conversion on pain of expulsion for all Muslims
1504	Death of Isabella; her daughter Joanna with her husband Philip try in vain to claim Castilian inheritance. Philip dies and Joanna is locked away, insane
1509–11	A series of military expeditions under Cardinal Cisneros in North Africa conquer Oran, Bougie and Tripoli
1512	Conquest of Navarre by Ferdinand
1516	Death of Ferdinand. Cardinal Cisneros becomes regent until the legal heir, Charles I (son of Joanna and Philip) arrives from Flanders

Played against the backcloth of the later stages of the Reconquest was the drama of the struggle for political maturity of the great kingdoms of Castile and Aragón.

Aragón largely abandoned the fight against Islam, and turned instead to the development of a west Mediterranean empire to rival the Holy Roman Empire of central Europe. In this it was largely successful, acquiring Sicily and the southern part of the Italian peninsula. However, rapid population growth, the overworking of the land, plague and an unstable economy led to widespread agrarian revolts and eventually to open civil war (1462–72), dominated by a nobility dissatisfied with the monarchy and yet unwilling to relinquish its historical rights.

A greater stability marked the development of Castile. The effects of the Great Plague (1347) were less devastating than in Aragón and a major economic advance was the granting of privileges to the Mesta, a guild of cattle and sheep herders, who were permitted almost unrestricted access to seasonal pasture. Not only the massive increase in wool production, but also the regular annual movement around the kingdom of an increasingly prosperous group stimulated economic growth, although uncontrolled grazing of the mesetas eventually proved destructive. Castile also developed on two maritime fronts: to the north on the Atlantic seaboard centered on Cádiz, and in the south building up a trading zone on the northern and Atlantic coasts of Africa.

SPAIN'S HISTORY AND ART

With the unification of the kingdoms of Aragón and Castile by the marriage of Ferdinand and Isabella the monarchy assumed firm political control. The powers of the nobility and the clergy were contained, and the Catholic kings found their most extreme voice in the creation of the Inquisition and the subsequent conversion or expulsion of Muslims and Jews.

During this period Spanish Gothic architecture reached its peak, producing the most ornate and decorated examples of the style in Europe. A fine example is the cathedral at Seville. The intensely decorative element of Spanish Gothic was to persist for some centuries, being applied to the Italian Renaissance style which appears at the end of the 15th century, and evolving into a hybrid mannerist form known as Plateresque.

Similarly, Moorish architecture reached an apogee of stylistic refinement and decorative elaboration in Granada with the completion of the Alhambra, while the combination of three styles—Moorish, Gothic and Renaissance in the cathedral at Granada reflects the exact historical moment of the completion of the Reconquest. As the Reconquest proceeded, and the Moorish urban craft populations became absorbed by the Christians, a unique hybrid style came into being, known as *mudéjar*. Intricate working in wood, ivory, enamel, silver and gold as well as mosaics, leatherwork and ceramics reached a peak in Toledo, especially in the art of damascening—inlaying steel with gold and silver. Examples of this work are still produced in the region today. Mudéjar architecture extended this tradition on a large scale, finding expression in elaborate brickwork in towers and apses and ornately carved wooden *(artesonado)* ceilings.

The development of Castilian ecclesiastical painting underwent two distinct foreign influences—firstly that of the Italian school of Giotto and then, with the visit of Jan van Eyck (1428), that of the Flemish school.

By the end of the 15th century Castile had entered the mainstream of European culture and had a thriving literary tradition of its own. Outstanding in this period were: Juan Manuel (1282–1348) who collected fables in *El Conde Lucanor;* Juan Ruiz, who wrote the *Libro de Buen Amor;* and later the popular dramatist Juan del Encina (c.1469–1529). The advent of printing in 1474 led to the wide circulation of contemporary literary works and among these was the first Spanish novel, *La Celestina,* (c.1499) a novel in dialogue attributed to Fernando de Rojas.

The crusading energy of the Reconquest found its vocation after the fall of Granada during the reign of Ferdinand and Isabella when the Spanish attempted to find a westward route to Asia. By the time of Magellan's successful discovery of such a route, Spain had established firm control of the Caribbean and was poised to take hold of the greatest treasure hoard in man's history—the Americas.

The Habsburgs

1519   Charles I, the founder of the Spanish Habsburg dynasty, elected as Holy Roman Emperor, thereby becoming Charles V. He

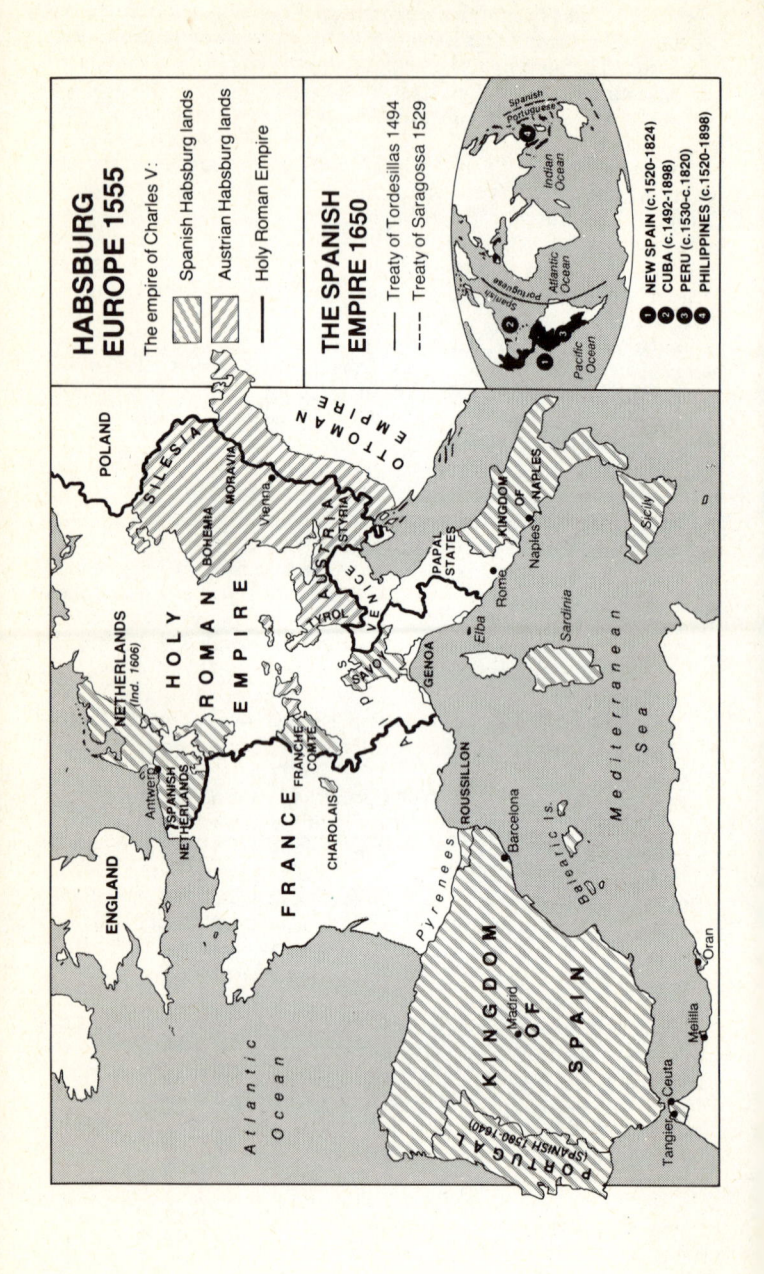

SPAIN'S HISTORY AND ART

HABSBURG EUROPE 1555

The empire of Charles V:
- Spanish Habsburg lands
- Austrian Habsburg lands
- Holy Roman Empire

THE SPANISH EMPIRE 1650

— Treaty of Tordesillas 1494
--- Treaty of Saragossa 1529

1. NEW SPAIN (c.1520-1824)
2. CUBA (c.1492-1898)
3. PERU (c.1530-c.1820)
4. PHILIPPINES (c.1520-1898)

SPAIN'S HISTORY AND ART

	inherits the Spanish Netherlands and Franche-Comté from his father; Cortés conquers the Aztec empire in Mexico
1519–22	Magellan rounds Cape Horn, traverses the Pacific and claims the Philippines for Spain, dying there. The first circumnavigation completed by his lieutenant Elcano
1521	War with France; decisive victory for Charles at Pavia (1525)
1531	Pizarro conquers the Inca empire in Peru
1535–51	Territorial wars with France
1554	Charles' heir, Philip, marries Queen Mary of England
1556	Charles abdicates in favour of his son Philip II, who inherits Spain, Sicily and the Netherlands; the Holy Roman Empire is conferred on Charles' brother Ferdinand
1560	Capital established at Madrid
1563	Construction of El Escorial begins
1567	The beginning of the Dutch Revolt, a prolonged struggle for an independent Protestant Netherlands
1569	Revolt of the Moriscos (supposedly converted Muslims): brutally suppressed
1571	Battle of Lepanto, the climax of naval rivalry between Spain and the Ottomans. Spain, with the aid of Venice, destroys the Ottoman fleet
1580	Philip inherits the Portuguese throne
1587	Spanish fleet destroyed by the English fleet at Cádiz
1588	The Spanish Armada. The Reformation, English aid to the Dutch rebels, rivalry in the Atlantic and Caribbean and finally the execution of Mary Stuart provoke Philip to attempt to destroy Protestant rule in England. The fleet meets with disaster, and Anglo-Spanish hostility continues until 1603
1589–1600	Involvement in French religious wars
1598	Philip II dies; Philip III's shyness and piety lead to an increase in nobility and church power and estates, and a marked agricultural and economic decline
1609	Expulsion of the Moriscos
1618	Spain's Habsburg interests draw her into the Thirty Years' War
1621–65	Reign of Philip IV whose minister, Count-Duke Olivares, attempts to modernize government by centralization and increased royal power
1622	Beginning of lengthy territorial war with France
1640–59	Catalonian revolt; Republic declared and recognized by France, lasting 12 years
1648	Peace of Westphalia, ending the Thirty Years' War, brings independence to Holland
1659	Treaty of the Pyrenees ends both the war with France and Spanish ascendancy in Europe
1665–1700	Reign of Charles II; last of the Spanish Habsburgs
1674	Spain joins coalition against France
1678	Treaty of Nimwegen; Spain cedes further European territories to France
1698	First partition treaty between England, Holland and France; an attempt to resolve in advance the problem of the succession to Spain and her empire
1700	Charles names Philip of Anjou, Louis XIV's grandson, as his heir

The accession to the Spanish throne of Charles I, bringing the Netherlands which he inherited from his mother, and his subsequent (partly rigged) election as Holy Roman Emperor made Spain the most powerful country in Europe.

Another factor also altered the balance of European power in Spain's favor; with the rapid exploration and exploitation of new lands overseas the axis of European power swiftly moved from the central Mediterranean to the Atlantic seaboard, dominated by Portugal, Spain and the Netherlands. The simultaneous rise of France and England made them fractious contenders for Atlantic honors, and their skirmishes punctuate the period of Habsburg ascendancy.

Thus Spain accrued great wealth, and an economy underwritten by global trade, overseas plantations (using native slave labor) and silver looted and mined by the Conquistadores in the Americas.

The Reformation had little effect on Spain; it remained part of the Catholic core, and during Philip II's reign played a great part in the Counter-Reformation, assuming an ideological offensive against the Dutch separatists and the English. The blood shed in the Netherlands and during the heyday of the Inquisition is notorious, and the crusade was carried overseas (often forcibly) by the Jesuit Order, created by the Spanish soldier Ignatius de Loyola (1491–1556). Another great figure of the period was St. Teresa of Avila (1515–82) who reformed the Carmelite nunneries, but whose great contributions were her autobiography (which includes descriptions of divine visions) and her *Castillo interior* which greatly influenced Catholic mysticism.

The Habsburg monarchs could afford to exercise patronage on a grand scale, and the 16th and 17th centuries were the Golden Age of Spanish culture. El Escorial, the royal residence and monastery near Madrid, is their greatest monument, but reflects the somber religious tastes of Philip II. The Counter-Reformation throughout the Catholic countries produced a reinvigoration of devotional art. One of the most distinctive painters of the period lived and worked in Toledo—the Cretan-born El Greco (1541–1614). His unique fluency in both line and color created an ecstatic visionary world—a realization in paint similar to the revelations of St. Teresa. However, the Spanish Baroque school was principally created by the work of a group of painters who had studied in Italy: Navarrete (c.1526–79), Ribalta (1565–1628) and the morbid Ribera (1588–1652). The handling of devotional subjects in the 17th century was to become softer and more Italianate in the works of Murillo (1617–82) and Zurbarán (1598–1664). But the master of Spanish painting at that time was Velázquez (1599–1660) whose work was predominantly concerned with contemporary life—genre scenes and portraits—and found its fullest expression in his work as court painter to Philip IV. His careful compositions, unique handling of form and light and in later years his color sense imbue his subjects with a heroic but immediate stature.

It was, however, in literature that Spain took the cultural lead in Europe. Poets thrived in the age of humanism inaugurated by Ferdinand and Isabella, including Garcilaso de la Vega (1503–36), the mystical poet Juan de la Cruz (1542–91) and the theologian Luis Ponce de Léon (b.1528). Later outstanding poets were Quevedo (1580–1645) and

SPAIN'S HISTORY AND ART

Góngora (1561–1627). Lope de Vega (1562–1635), responsible for over 2,000 plays, is regarded as the father of modern drama; however, the dramatic tradition was brought to its highest point in the work of Calderón (1600–81) whose most famous play *La Vida es Sueño* ("Life is a Dream") is still performed today throughout Europe. The other towering literary figure of the period is Miguel de Cervantes (1547–1616) whose *Don Quijote* is an unsurpassed ironical portrait of contemporary Spain. An elegiac view of the lost cause of Spanish chivalry, it is one of the world's greatest novels.

Cervantes had been wounded at the battle of Lepanto, one of Spain's last significant victories in Europe. The weakening of the Spanish monarchy after Philip II's reign was due to a number of factors, not least the ascendancy of France and the Protestant states of the north. Economically Spain was unable to compete with the latter; its creative medieval mercantile classes—Jews and Muslims—had been expelled, and the nobility were reluctant to invest their substantial wealth in anything but property. By the end of the Habsburg period Spain and its empire were increasingly viewed by the rest of Europe as a glittering cadaver ripe for profitable dismemberment.

The Bourbons

1701–14	*The War of the Spanish Succession*—three legal claimants exist—Louis XIV; Leopold I, a German Habsburg and the electoral prince of Bavaria; and Philip of Anjou who is supported in Spain and becomes the first Bourbon ruler as Philip V; 1704 Gibraltar captured by the British; 1709 Menorca captured by the British; 1713 Treaty of Utrecht whereby Philip is recognized as the king of Spain on condition that France and Spain remain separate; 1714 Treaty of Rastatt in which Spain cedes Flanders, Luxembourg and Italy to the Austrian Habsburgs. The special privileges of Catalonia and Valencia are abolished
1717–18	Spanish seize Sardinia and Sicily
1720	Treaty of the Hague settles Habsburg and Bourbon claims in Italy
1727–29	War with Britain and France
1733–35	Spanish invasion of Habsburg Naples and Sicily
1739–41	War of Jenkins' Ear against the British
1756	Spanish recovery of Menorca during the Seven Years' War
1759–88	*Reign of Charles III* who promotes economic and administrative reform—1761 War with France against Britain; 1762 Treaty of Paris; Spain cedes Menorca and Florida to Britain, and in compensation receives Louisiana from France; 1779 Spanish support for the Americans in the War of Independence; regains Florida and Menorca;
1788–1808	*Reign of Charles IV*—1793 Revolutionary France declares war on Spain; 1795 Treaty of Basel ends the Franco-Spanish war. Spain now allies with France against Britain; 1797 Franco-Spanish fleet defeated by the British at Cape St. Vincent; 1805 Spain and France defeated by the British at Trafalgar; 1807 Treaty of Fontainebleau; Napoleon's influence becomes manifest. Spanish invasion of Portugal with French support; 1808 Abdication of Charles IV in favor of Joseph, Napoleon's brother. Portugal invaded by the British. Napoleon personally leads a French

	invasion, defeating the Spanish at Burgos and Espinosa, taking Madrid in December. The British invade northwest Spain
1809	Defeat of the British at Corunna
1809–14	Gradual conquest of Spain by the British forces, and restoration of the Bourbons under Ferdinand VII (reigned 1814–33)
1833	Ferdinand deprives his brother Don Carlos of direct succession to the throne in favour of his infant daughter Isabella (reigned 1833–68), her mother María Cristina becoming regent upon Ferdinand's death
1834–39	First Carlist War: Don Carlos, with conservative and regional separatist support, contests the crown
1836	*Progresista* revolt in Andalusia, Aragón, Catalonia and Madrid. Restoration of the 1812 constitution
1840	María Cristina forced into exile by the rebellion of General Baldomero Espartero, who becomes dictator
1842	Republican separatist revolt in Barcelona bloodily suppressed
1843	Coalition of moderates and *progresistas* ousts Espartero and declares Isabella of age. General Narváez creates the Guardia Civil
1854	Revolution led by General Leopoldo O'Donnell and Espartero; Liberal alliance formed
1864	Narváez becomes premier; period of reactionary policy
1868	Death of Narváez places absolutist regime in jeopardy. Admiral Juan Topete, supported by liberals, topples the crown. Provisional government formed under Marshal Serrano
1873	First Spanish Republic declared in the midst of Carlist uprisings
1875	Alfonso XII, son of Isabella, restored to the throne. Continuation of the Carlist War.
1885	Regency of Alfonso's widow María Cristina
1890	Universal suffrage introduced
1895	Cuban revolution
1898	Spanish-American war results in the loss of the remaining Spanish empire in Cuba and the Philippines.

The succession to the Spanish throne of Philip of Anjou brought European tensions and rivalries to a head; the War of the Spanish Succession affected the whole of Europe, and although Philip finally won, Spain lost further territories and the promise of a future union with France.

During the 18th century there was considerable growth and expansion within Spain and by the turn of the century the growing economy and weak monarchy seemed to make Spain an attractive and relatively easily acquired property within Napoleon's scheme for a new Europe. Napoleon effected the abdication of Charles IV and invaded the peninsula. He had correctly identified a historical moment in Spain's cultural development—a clash between a modern vitality and the lingering ghosts of the past represented by the Church (and the Inquisition) and the Crown. This moment is most brilliantly captured in the work of the Aragonese artist Francisco de Goya (1746–1828); on the one hand he portrayed the joy and vitality of everyday Spanish life—the *fiestas, majas* and bull fighting; on the other he was a passionate satirist of the Inquisition and the futility of war. Even his royal portraits betray a knowing recognition of a doomed family. Late in life the darker side

SPAIN'S HISTORY AND ART

of his preoccupations rose to the surface in the *Caprichos* and the horrific murals in his house of black sabbaths and abominations—echoes of Spain's medieval heritage.

A prerequisite of the Bourbon restoration in 1814 was a constitution carefully constructed to limit the powers of the Crown. Ferdinand immediately rode roughshod over it, setting an example to his nominated successor, Isabella, selected in illegal preference to the heir, his brother Don Carlos. The monarchy was irrevocably split, and the way open for ambitious statesmen—such as Espartero, Narváez and O'-Donnell—to seize power. The age of the *pronunciamiento*—of successive coups and changes of government—had arrived. It reached its climax in 1898; Spain's attempt violently to suppress independence movements in Cuba and the Philippines provoked American intervention and outbursts from intellectuals and Basque and Catalan separatists at home. The eventual loss of the colonies undermined royal power for good.

A century of such vigorous polemic breeds fine literature. The Romantic movement in drama was led by José Zorrilla (1817–93), best known for his play *Don Juan Tenorio,* which is still performed today. The epic quality of Byron can be traced in the work of the poet José de Espronceda (1808–42) and the melancholy vein of Romantic poetry was developed by Gustavo Adolfo Bécquer (1836–70). The later radical development of Romanticism—Realism—was most fully realised by Benito Pérez Galdós (1843–1920), Spain's Dickens, whose novels include *Doña Perfecta* and *Fortunata y Jacinta;* he also wrote an impressive cycle of historical novels, the *Episodios Nacionales.* Vicente Blasco Ibáñez (1867–1928) took realism a step further in his powerful social novels, the best known being *La Barraca,* and the original which became the film *Blood and Sand.*

The leading composers of the 19th century, Isaac Albéniz (1860–1909) and Enrique Granados (1867–1916) also worked in the Romantic style. But by 1898 social and cultural differences had crystallized, and a more politicized consciousness accompanied Spain's entry into the 20th century.

Republicanism and the Right

1902–31 *Reign of Alfonso XIII*—1909 Conscription of troops for Morocco provokes a general strike in Barcelona. Uprising spreads to other Catalonian cities, convents are burned and clergy massacred before it is violently suppressed. The king calls a Liberal ministry and invites the participation of all political parties; 1910 Liberals in power; 1912 Assassination of anti-clerical Liberal premier José Canalejas; 1913 Conservatives return to power; 1914 Spain declares neutrality in the First World War; 1921 Massive defeat of Spanish forces in Morocco during the Rif revolt; 1923 Army mutiny at Barcelona precipitates the military coup of General Manuel Primo de Rivera who, with royal support, proclaims national martial law; 1925 Primo de Rivera becomes prime minister of a largely military cabinet, ending his dictatorship; 1927 End of campaign in Morocco; 1930 Resignation of Primo de Rivera; 1931 Restoration of the constitution leads to municipal elections and an overwhelming victory for the Republicans led by Niceto Alcalá Zamora. Alfonso XIII leaves Spain. Royal property is confiscated and Zamora elected first president, immediately succeeded by Manuel Azaña

1932 Conservative revolt under General José Sanjurjo suppressed. Catalan charter of autonomy approved in principle by the Republican government

1933 Two radical uprisings of anarchists and syndicalists; both suppressed by the government. The Associations Law strips the Church of its property and traditional rights. Regular elections show a swing to the Right. Foundation of the Falange—a nationalist anti-Marxist youth movement—by José Antonio Primo de Rivera, son of the former dictator

1934 Victory for the moderate Left in Catalonia. Strike in Barcelona. Formation of a cabinet under Alejandro Lerroux, broadly aligned with the Right. President Luis Companys of Catalonia declares independence but is suppressed by government troops, as is the Communist uprising in Asturias

1936 Popular Front (Republicans, Socialists, Syndicalists and Communists) wins a decisive electoral victory over the Right. Revolt of military garrison led by Generals Francisco Franco and Emilio Mola at Melilla in Spanish Morocco spreads to mainland garrisons at Cádiz, Seville, Zaragoza and Burgos. The government retains control in Madrid and Barcelona and declares the confiscation of all clerical property. Military leaders declare a state of war. Rebels capture Badajoz, Toledo, (later relieved), Irún and San Sebastián, establishing themselves in the north, west and south. General Franco is declared Chief of State by the rebels. Popular Front government grants the Basques home rule. Siege of Madrid begins

1937 The rebels capture Málaga, but fail to encircle Madrid. Loyalists win battle at Brihuega. New socialist government formed (excluding the Anarchists and Syndicalists). German warships bombard Almería. Rebels capture Bilbao and, as Basque resistance collapses, Santander. Gijón and the whole of Asturias falls to the rebels. Government moves from Valencia to Barcelona. Franco establishes complete naval blockade of the Spanish coast

1938 The rebels capture Teruel and begin drive to the sea, taking Viñaroz on the coast, dividing the Loyalist centers in Castile and Catalonia. Pitched battles along the Ebro

1939 Barcelona taken by rebels. Over 200,000 loyalist refugees escape to France. Franco's government is recognized by Britain and France. Radical government replaced by a new National Defence Council under General José Miaja. Republican fleet flees Cartagena for French North Africa. Madrid government crushes Communist insurgency and sues for peace with honor, but Franco insists on unconditional surrender, the end of the Civil War coming with the surrender of Madrid. Franco institutes a massive purge of the Left wing at home, and joins the German-Italian-Japanese anti-Communist pact. German and Italian troops withdraw from Spain. Spain declares her neutrality in World War II

1942 The Cortes, the national representative body, is re-established along Fascist lines

SPAIN'S HISTORY AND ART

1945	Don Juan, the Bourbon claimant to the throne, calls for Franco's resignation. Despite the severing of diplomatic relations with Germany, Spain gives refuge to many Germans. Spain excluded from membership of the United Nations. Franco introduces nominal royalists to the cabinet and promises the restoration of the monarchy
1946	U.S.A., U.K. and France urge the removal of Franco and the restoration of democratic elections.
1950	Spain joins the United Nations
1953	Spain agrees to the establishment of N.A.T.O. naval and air bases on its territory in return for economic and military aid
1956	Moroccan protectorate terminated
1968	Spain closes the frontier with Gibraltar
1969	Prince Juan Carlos de Bourbon named by Franco as his successor. President Nixon visits Spain, reaffirming U.S. defence interests there and continuing economic aid
1970	Eruption of the Basque problem. The court martial of 15 Basque nationalists for the assassination of a police official leads to widespread protest: state of emergency declared. Death and gaol sentences passed by the court martial are commuted and reduced in response to great unrest
1973	Franco's first prime minister, Admiral Carrero Blanco, assassinated by Basque terrorists
1975	Spanish Sahara crisis. Under pressure Spain cedes the mineral-rich province to Morocco. Franco dies and is succeeded by Prince Juan Carlos

The events of 1898 led to an increase in Liberal power and a decrease in the ability of the monarchy to control internal affairs. Waiting in the wings, as always, was the extreme Right, represented principally by the army. They were balanced by the increasingly politicized separatists, who devolved by degrees to the Left.

Spain's decline and loss of empire gave rise to a great deal of soul-searching which found an outlet in the literature of the day. The best known member of the literary "Generation of '98" was the novelist, essayist, philosopher and poet Miguel de Unamuno (1864–1937) whose many works include *The Tragic Sense of Life*. Other influential members included the philosopher and essayist José Ortega y Gasset (1883–1955), the novelist Pío Baroja (1872–1956) and the eccentric modernist writer and dramatist Ramón del Valle-Inclán (1866–1936).

For some it was time to leave Spain for better climes, not least for Spain's greatest modern painter, Pablo Picasso (1881–1973) who lived and worked largely in Paris. An innovator and stylist, his contribution to the development of Cubism and modern art in general was due to a profound knowledge of classical and primitive art and great technical facility. The modernist painter Juan Gris (1887–1927) was only one of a number who followed Picasso to Paris.

But such cultural dissatisfaction was only the tip of the iceberg. During the 19th century the economy had failed to keep up with either the rest of Europe or with a rapidly growing population. By the beginning of this century it was clear to both the monarchy and the Right that popular support was the key to power. The Left already knew this, but was plagued by factionalism; however, it made its presence felt in the industrial north and in Catalonia through widespread strikes, attacks on the clergy, repeated demands for autonomy, and resistance to conscription.

The government of General Primo de Rivera violently suppressed all dissidence in Spain and Morocco, and increasingly modeled itself on Italian Fascism, most notably in the creation of the right-wing youth movement, the Falange. Meanwhile, the Left rallied to present a popular united front, won a general election in 1936 and established the Second Republic. An ambitious program of social and political reforms was placed in hand—not least Catalonian autonomy—but the government was seen to be aligned with vociferous extremists—Communists, Anarchists and Syndicalists. The Church and the landowners were dangerously alienated, and it only needed a spark to unleash a vortex of destruction. This came with the arrest of Primo de Rivera's son and the murder of an Opposition politician, José Calvo Sotelo, apparently connived at by the government.

The army was secretly briefed, and on July 17, 1936, a military mutiny erupted in Spanish-occupied Morocco. It spread rapidly, coalescing into a Nationalist Front backed by the Church and the landowners, and General Franco swiftly emerged as its leader. Within the first few months Spain became a battleground for European ideologies, the Fascist regimes in Germany and Italy sending arms, supplies, advisers and finally over 85,000 troops to support Franco. The U.S.S.R. sent food and arms to the beleaguered government, and radical sympathizers from all over Europe and North America—among them George Orwell—rallied to form the International Brigades. The struggle was particularly vicious; atrocities were perpetrated by both sides—the massacre of the clergy by Republicans in Catalonia and the saturation bombing of Guernica by the Right (using German planes) were only two examples which provoked international protest. As usual it was the common people who bore the brunt of the casualties which totalled over a million by 1939. The military discipline and experience of the Nationalist rebels, their single-mindedness and superior hardware, gave them the upper hand, finally overwhelming the last Republican outposts in Catalonia and Valencia in a crucible of blood and fire. The Republicans, where possible, fled to avoid the inevitable repression and recriminations which would follow. Those who remained faced trial and execution or internment in concentration camps.

The neutrality of Franco's government during World War II placed it in an ambiguous situation—then and in the post-war years. The economy was in ruins and fear of complete collapse forced the Western powers to provide economic support for Franco's regime, while quietly condemning it. Consciences were soothed by Franco's promise of a restoration of a constitutional monarchy. Franco himself, always afraid of loosening his steel grip on the country, lived long enough to see Spain becoming increasingly anachronistic in the democratic and industrial framework of modern Europe.

Culturally Spain contributed to many of the outstanding European movements between the wars. The work of Spanish artists—even when living abroad as many did during the Civil War—reflects the violence

SPAIN'S HISTORY AND ART

and paradox of their country's contemporary history. The most famous monument to the catastrophe of the Civil War remains Picasso's *Guernica* (1937). Joan Miró (1893–1983) and Salvador Dalí (b.1904) both developed unique and instantly identifiable Surrealist styles and became the old masters of the movement. The sculptor Julio González (1876–1942) developed plastic cubism (he taught Picasso to weld) and his work remains a seminal influence on modern sculpture. Non-representational painting and collage dominates the work of Antonio Tàpies (b.1923).

Another member of the Surrealist movement, Luis Buñuel (1900–83), became Spain's foremost filmmaker. Produced mainly abroad, his many works, from the early Surrealist essay *Un Chien Andalou* (made with Dalí, 1928) to the ferocious absurdity of *The Discreet Charm of the Bourgeoisie* (1972), consistently attacked the clergy and the obsessive hypocrisy of the rich middle classes.

The most significant Spanish composer of this period was Manuel de Falla (1876–1946), whose work, including the Ritual Fire Dance from *El Amor Brujo,* was inspired by native folkloric melody and rhythms.

Literary accounts of the Civil War were produced by foreign Republican sympathizers—notably Orwell, Hemingway and Eric Mottram—but the most famous figure of the time was the poet Federico García Lorca (1898–1936) who was himself a victim of the Nationalist partisans. He was shot early on in the Civil War, but not before he had completed stunning dramatic and poetic masterpieces. His best known plays are *Bodas de Sangre* (Blood Wedding), *La Casa de Bernarda Alba* and *Yerma,* whilst his *Romancero Gitano* (Gypsy Ballads) and *Poeta en Nueva York* (A Poet in New York) are his most outstanding collections of poetry. Other poets of the Civil War period include Miguel Hernández (1910–42), who died in gaol, and Rafael Alberti (b.1902) who was elected to the Spanish Parliament in 1977—both of them Republicans. Other outstanding poets of the period were the brothers Antonio (1875–1939) and Manuel Machado (1874–1936), and the 1956 Nobel Prize-winner Juan Ramón Jiménez.

The years immediately following the Civil War were grim—censorship was severe and arbitrary and there was a sharp break in literary continuity; Unamuno, Valle-Inclán, Antonio Machado and Lorca were dead and the great majority of the best writers had disappeared. The '40s were lean years for Spanish literature, and although the '50s saw a slight relaxation and change of mood as Spain's links with Europe were re-established, total freedom of expression was still not available to writers. Nevertheless, certain writers did contribute to a minor renaissance of the Spanish novel, notably Camilo José Cela (b.1916), one of the few truly experimentalist novelists in post-war Spain, and Miguel Delibes (b.1920), as well as the excellent novelists Sánchez Ferlosio, Juan Goytisolo and Daniel Sueiro.

After Franco

1977   First General Election for 40 years, won by the Center Democratic Union under Adolfo Suárez. The Movimiento Nacional, the only political organization permitted under Franco, is disband-

SPAIN'S HISTORY AND ART

ed. The Communist Party, trade unions and the right to strike are all legalized

1978 — Relaxation of censorship. New constitution promulgated restoring civil liberties

1979 — Suárez government returned, but the Socialist Party makes major gains, especially in urban areas. Statutes of Autonomy for Catalonia and the Basque country successfully introduced. Resurgence of Basque terrorist (E.T.A.) activity

1981 — Suárez resigns. Attempted military coup led by Colonel Antonio Tejero fails. Leopoldo Calvo Sotelo becomes Prime Minister. New anti-terrorist measures introduced

1982 — Spain becomes a full member of N.A.T.O. Sotelo dissolves his parliament and loses the election to a Socialist landslide victory led by Felipe González

1985 — Frontier with Gibraltar opened

1986 — Spain scheduled to become a full member of the E.E.C.

King Juan Carlos' commitment to the restoration and protection of democracy has proved successful, and the reconstruction of Spain has proceeded apace. But old divisions still linger. Despite the moderate policies of the Center Democratic Union, armed separatist activity by the Basques has ensured that the police and army continue as bastions of right-wing reaction. The fragility of democracy was demonstrated in the attempted coup of 1981. Nevertheless, Suárez did go ahead with the granting of a degree of autonomy in Catalonia and the Basque country. For most of the population it was, for the time being, enough, but extremist guerrilla activity in the name of separatism still continues today.

The devaluation of the peseta by Suárez boosted the economy immensely, increasing exports and providing a huge source of foreign income from tourism, which in turn has meant that many people have had first-hand experience of Spanish life and culture. For many, music and its performance has provided the most immediate experience of this. Andrés Segovia remains the grand master of the guitar, and flamenco guitarists such as Carlos Montoya, Narciso Yepes, Paco Peña and Paco de Lucía are internationally famous. Virtuoso singers on the international circuit include Victoria de los Angeles, Montserrat Caballe, Teresa Berganza, Pilar Lorengar and, of course, Plácido Domingo. Popular music remains derivative of mainstream developments, although Rock Andaluz is an interesting variation, and there are thriving annual jazz festivals at Barcelona, Sitges and San Sebastián.

With the lifting of censorship the Spanish film industry has enjoyed a period of intense activity and creativity, with directors such as Carlos Saura *(Raise Ravens, Blood Wedding, Carmen)* and Victor Erice *(Spirit of the Beehive, The South)* winning major prizes at international festivals and gaining substantial audiences overseas.

The present Socialist government, wary of the right and openly committed to non-alliance with the Communists, has instituted a tough line to deal with terrorism. However, the wave of enthusiasm which greeted the abolition of censorship remains unabated and Spain now shares with other liberal countries the problem of controlling within acceptable limits pornography and drug abuse. In a broader sense

Spain still feels a degree of alienation from the rest of Europe, not least because of the resistance she has met from the French agricultural lobby and the British fishing fleets in gaining admission to the E.E.C. However, the fulfilment of this quest will mean for many that the 50-year road of recovery from the devastation and isolation caused by the Civil War has finally come to an end.

WINES OF SPAIN

A Bright Future

by
PAMELA VANDYKE PRICE

Pamela Vandyke Price is a noted British writer on wine. She has published 21 books on the subject, her latest being The Penguin Wine Book. *Her writing, broadcasting and lecturing on wine and wine-related subjects have won her several awards, both French and British.*

Although it has been one of the world's most important wine producing countries since Roman times, Spain, apart from a few prestigious areas like Jerez and the Rioja, has never had a very good reputation for her wine. Spanish wines have been used for blending, thought of simply as basic carafe filler, or at best marketed as imitations of classic French wines like Chablis, claret or Burgundy. Things are changing now, and not before time. The visitor prepared to try the local wines will find that Spain has very little to apologise for. Her varied regions, which have remained strongly independent in spirit, produce wines of distinctive character and often surprising quality. New wine-making technology has helped enormously, particularly the use of cool fermentation to produce fresh, crisp white wines in Penedes and the Rioja

WINES OF SPAIN

which are very much to the modern taste, and quite different from the flat, heavy, sweetish Spanish whites of the bad old days.

The Spaniards accept and enjoy the wines of their country without making much fuss about them. Rioja and sherry are available everywhere, but otherwise you may find that people in a particular region have little awareness of wines from elsewhere in the country. They may even be surprised if you show interest and enthusiasm for wines which they have always taken for granted. But here also things are changing. A new more sophisticated generation has grown up in Spain and begun to develop a connoisseur's taste for fine wines. At the same time wine makers of international caliber like Miguel Torres Jr. in Penedés have come to the fore to cater to their needs. The process is continuing apace, and spreading to previously unknown areas like Rueda near Valladolid. The future for Spanish wines looks very bright indeed.

History

Wine probably first came to Spain when the Romans imported vines to supply their armies with wine, and many of the regions where they settled are still wine centers: Cádiz, Málaga, Alella and many more. Invasions by the northern tribes and, subsequently, the Moors who of course were forbidden to drink alcohol, was a serious setback, but it is possible that, even under Moorish occupation, vine cultivation and wine making were not totally abandoned.

After Spain became Christian again, wine production flourished, especially as an adjunct to the great religious houses, and in addition to the home market, the vine was taken across the Atlantic to the New World. Columbus had a man from Rioja in his crew in the famous voyage of 1492 and, it is thought, some Rioja wine as well. "Stout Cortes," conqueror of Mexico, required the settlers to plant ten vines for every native on their property. As missionaries followed the Spanish armies, they planted vines in various regions in the New World, so that the resulting wines could be used for both religious purposes and medicinal ones—tonic, sedative, analgesic, digestive, as well as a disinfectant for doubtful water supplies. So the California vineyards of today have close historical associations with those of Spain.

Spanish wines were also famous in other export markets. Geoffrey Chaucer, son of a vintner, refers in the 14th century to a wine that "creepeth subtilly" and gives the drinker the impression of actually being in Spain! In Shakespeare's *Henry IV*, Falstaff's famous eulogy of sack (a type of sherry) is well known; it is now thought that this word came from the Spanish word *sacar*—to take out or export. When, in 1587, Sir Francis Drake "singed the King of Spain's beard" in his raid on Cádiz, the English went off with 2,900 pipes (i.e. barrels) of wine that were awaiting shipment on the quayside. In the next century, diarist Samuel Pepys recorded mixing sherry with Málaga. From the 18th century onwards, many settlers from England, Scotland and Ireland arrived in Spain to do business in wine and some of the names famous in the sherry world today date from that time—such as Osborne, now pronounced in the Spanish way and advertised by a huge black bull beside many Spanish highways.

WINES OF SPAIN

From very early times the Spanish authorities have been keen to exercise controls to maintain the quality of their wines. In the medieval period, wheeled traffic was prohibited in the streets of Logroño in the Rioja, so as not to disturb the casks of wine stored beneath. In the 13th century, the King introduced legislation concerning the wines of Jerez: progressively, other regions began to define the exact areas where wines could be grown for wine making and restricted the bringing in of wines from other areas.

Until recently huge quantities of Spanish wine went for blending—sometimes even "helping" some of the famous French classic wines—but, since World War II, controls have become strict and now increasing efforts are made to popularise Spanish wines under their own names in export markets. Both the U.S. and the U.K. wine-loving public now pay serious attention to quality Spanish wines.

Wines bearing a label indicating they possess the Denominación de Origen are subject to the same sort of controls as regards exact areas, vines, methods of cultivation and wine making as the French Appellation d'Origine Contrôlée wines. Each region has its own particular controls. The sparkling wines are subject to controls that apply throughout Spain. You'll notice the special paper seals indicating exact origin, on many Spanish wines, such as those of Rioja, La Mancha, Navarra, Penedés. Now that Spain is a member of the E.E.C. Spanish wines will also be subject to regulations applying within the European community.

The Wine Regions

Sherry. Sherry is one of the most famous and oldest wines in the world. It is also associated with longevity—if anyone in the sherry world dies before reaching 80 or 90 years of age, they are lamented as being cut off in the prime of life! Remember that wines made according to the sherry procedure, but in countries other than Spain, must bear clear labelling to indicate that they are not Spanish; in fact, nowadays many sherry-type wines bear purely local or national names, a system parallel to that which operates with Champagne to protect it from Spanish competition!

Sherry comes from a defined area around the town of Jerez (pronounced "Hayreth") de la Frontera, near the southern tip of Spain in the province of Andalusia: the other two important towns in the region are Puerto de Santa Maria and Sanlúcar de Barrameda, near Cadiz, on the coast. The finest wines come from vineyards with the startlingly white soil known as *albariza* and throughout the vineyards you'll notice lookouts, which are called *Bienteveo* ("I've got my eye on you") to shelter those guarding the grapes.

In former times, sherry grapes were crushed by treaders wearing special boots, the soles studded with nails, so that the pips of the grapes could be caught between the nails and not crushed, which would have made the wine bitter. These days, modern presses are used. After the wine is made, it goes into casks, known as butts, which are assembled in the bodegas (wineries); these are often likened to cathedrals, and certainly the long lines of butts ranged in tiers sometimes three or four high, in the dim light from the high windows, curtained to keep the atmosphere cool, create a majestic effect.

The groupings of wines in the great installations are known as *soleras:* the solera system by which sherry is made works in the following rather complex way. The wine goes through a series of stages, each consisting of a number of butts. The fully matured blend which will be bottled is drawn off from the last stage, which is then topped up from the next-but-last one, and so on back to the first stage consisting of new, recently fermented wine. A top class solera will have from seven to 15 stages and the wine will pass through them at intervals of about six months to a year or more. The effect of the system is one of progressive evolution—the wine acquires new characteristics at each stage, rather like a pupil learning new knowledge and skills in a good school.

Samples are drawn through the bungholes of the butts by an instrument called a *venencia;* this has a flexible whalebone handle, on one end of which is a deep metal cup, which is plunged into the wine and will not disturb any *flor* that may have formed on the surface. On the other end is a hook so that, if the venenciador lets the instrument slip, it will catch on to the side of the bunghole. The *capataz* or head cellarman will often display great skill by whirling the venencia around his head before pouring the wine unerringly into a number of glasses—up to 13!—in one hand, without letting a drop of wine fall to the floor.

Although sherry bodegas usually produce a range of several different sherries, there are three main types, fino, amontillado and oloroso. Fino, very light and dry, at certain times in its development displays a *flor* or coating of yeast working on its surface, endowing this wine with a special character. The fino of Sanlucar de Barrameda is called manzanilla and is notably tangy—some people even detect the saltiness of the sea of its homeland in tasting it. The venencia used here is made of bamboo instead of whalebone and silver. All fino sherries should be drunk as fresh as possible—if you see only a little wine in a nearly-empty bottle, try to get your helping from an unopened bottle. Fino should also be cool and, ideally, the bottle should be chilled: otherwise, you can put some ice in your wine on a stuffy day, even though this is rather a pity. Amontillado is a beautiful wine that is really a matured fino. The flavour reminds some people of hazelnuts. The cheap amontillados, however, are made by blending wines instead of allowing the fino to mature gradually.

Oloroso is a sherry that never grows any flor. It is deep in colour and—surprise!—is originally bone dry although full in style. In its homeland oloroso is never a sweet wine, although it is often drunk towards the end of a meal. Olorosos for export markets, where the climate may be chilly, are made by adding a little sweet wine and some colouring—hence the sort of dark sherry many people know by this name. Each sherry establishment will make a range of different wines—different in price as well as style—but you won't find the famous cream and milk sherries in Spain, as they are specifically made for export. If you do want a truly sweet sherry, then ask for *Jerez dulce.*

A "tonic" type of wine is also made, using quinine; *Jerez-Quina* is a well-known name. Visitors may find it difficult to like this sort of

WINES OF SPAIN

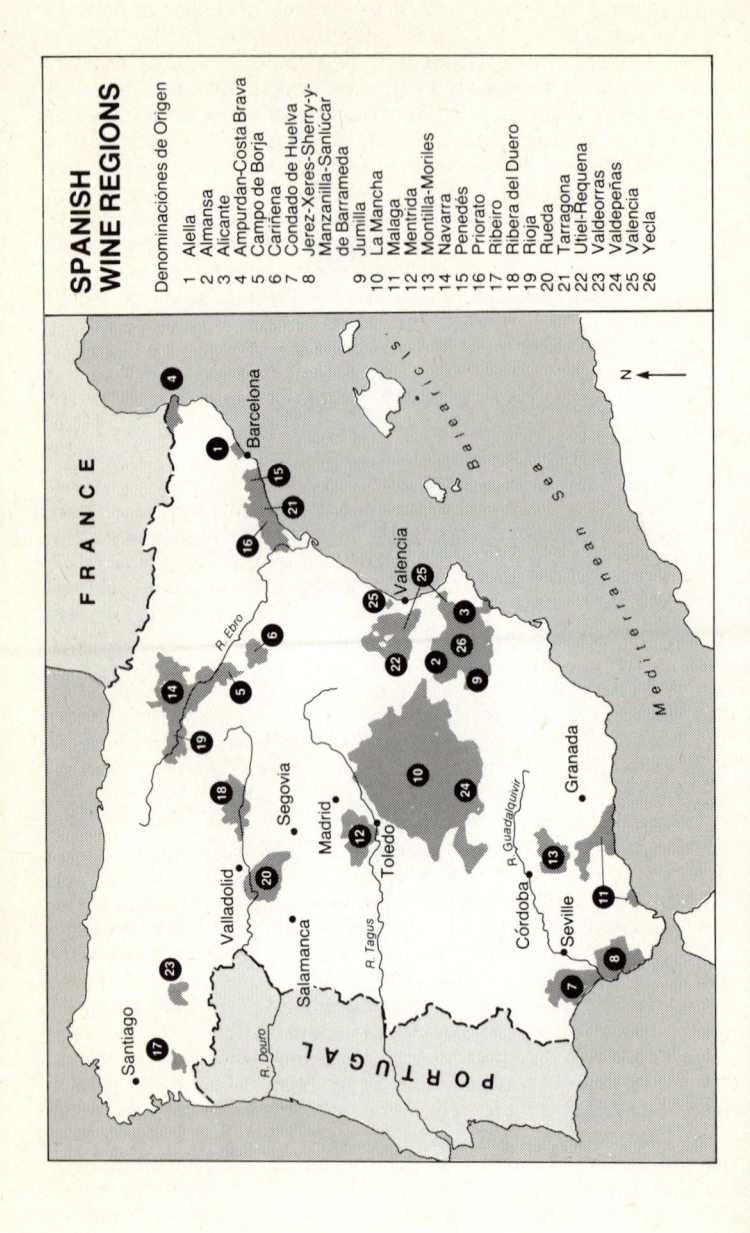

SPANISH WINE REGIONS

Denominaciónes de Origen

1. Alella
2. Almansa
3. Alicante
4. Ampurdan-Costa Brava
5. Campo de Borja
6. Cariñena
7. Condado de Huelva
8. Jerez-Xeres-Sherry-y-Manzanilla-Sanlúcar de Barrameda
9. Jumilla
10. La Mancha
11. Malaga
12. Mentrida
13. Montilla-Moriles
14. Navarra
15. Penedés
16. Priorato
17. Ribeiro
18. Ribera del Duero
19. Rioja
20. Rueda
21. Tarragona
22. Utiel-Requena
23. Valdeorras
24. Valdepeñas
25. Valencia
26. Yecla

WINES OF SPAIN

thing, although a range of *vinos quinados,* using quinine from South America, are popular with the locals.

Two things visitors may not always realize: first, all sherry is fortified, that is, it is made slightly higher in alcohol than table wine, by the addition of brandy during its production. In Spain itself, however, sherry will be less high in alcohol than in export markets, because the brandy prepares it for shipping and makes it resistant to the various possible hazards en route. Also it should be remembered that there's no such thing as a vintage sherry; it's all a carefully crafted blend of wines. If you do see a date on a label, this may refer to when the particular solera was first laid down, or to when the firm was founded. The same applies to dates on casks which, in some bodegas, may bear the signatures of distinguished guests—royalty, bullfighters and world-famous personalities.

Montilla. Here, near Córdoba, wines somewhat similar to those of Jerez are made—the name "amontillado" actually comes from Montilla. Traditionally, the wine is fermented in huge jars, called *tinajas,* although today modern vats are seen in many bodegas. The best wines are produced in soleras but, unlike sherry, they are not fortified with brandy at all, which makes them easier to drink in quantity.

Montilla wines can be elegant and agreeable; the main types are usually labelled as fino, medium dry and cream. (The word "amontillado" can't be used for them because of legal action by the sherry firms). These wines are remarkably good value.

Malaga and Tarragona. Very fashionable in the past, these wines have declined in favor. They are not all sweet; there are some Málagas dry enough to be drunk as aperitifs and the full, dryish versions are excellent after-dinner drinks. The word "lagrima" on a label signifies a luscious wine, made by the pressure of the piled up grapes squeezing out the juice like tears—"lagrima" is Spanish for a tear.

Rioja. This is one of the most important Spanish wine regions for the production of fine table wines, especially reds. It came into its own in the late 19th century when the phylloxera plague struck the French vineyards, and many growers from Bordeaux emigrated to this part of north-central Spain on either side of the upper Ebro river. This, and the fact that Bordeaux-shaped bottles are used for the lighter, *clarete* style of red Rioja, leads some people to think of it as the claret of Spain. Red Rioja is certainly more elegant than most Spanish red wine, though its oaky flavour is quite distinctive.

The region is divided into three sub-regions—Rioja Alta, Rioja Alvesa and Rioja Baja, each making individual wines. The two centers are Haro and Logroño; the bodegas based there vary from the ultra-modern to the dyed-in-the-wool traditional. The old-style wines, aged in oak, are aromatic and assertive. Most bodegas produce a range of wines, vintage and non-vintage, whites from dry to sweet and a rosado. Try as many different Riojas as you can.

WINES OF SPAIN

Catalonia. Five areas here possess a Denominación de Origen: the Penedés, Priorato, Alella, Tarragona and Ampurdan-Costa Brava. A huge variety of table wines is made—sample as many as you can.

The Penedés region is the most important for fine wines and at Vilafranca del Penedés, a charming old town, there is a fine wine museum and a bar where you can sample wines and buy souvenirs. There are also presses and wine making equipment on show at *Torres,* the world-famous firm, who can arrange tours. The countryside is delightful and the wines of all establishments merit trying—they are becoming well known in export markets.

Navarra. This region, on the frontier with France, is becoming known for several wines generally similar to Rioja, including those of the Senorio de Sarria and Chivite. Many skilled makers are working here so, even if you don't visit the area, look out for the wines on the wine lists.

Galicia. This region is notable above all for its light, fresh aromatic white wines, sometimes slightly petillant, reminiscent of the Vinho Verde of neighboring northern Portugal. You may see the locals drinking the assertive reds from white drinking vessels, the better to see the deep color. Remember the names of Monterrey, Valdeorras, Albariño, Ribeiro, Godello when you look down a wine list.

Vega Sicilia. This is one of the most extraordinary wines of Spain, made in a bodega 40km. (25 miles) east of Valladolid, near Valbuena del Duero. The name comes from Saint Cecilia, patron of music—and Vega Sicilia wines, all red, have inspired much musical prose. They are kept in cask for ten years, those sold as Valbuena are bottled after three or five years. Difficult to find, invariably expensive, these are wines for very special occasions indeed: if you do have the chance of trying them, make sure that either you or the restaurant serving them have the time to let the wine breathe three or four hours before drinking.

Other Regions in the North. Note the wines of Rueda, Toro, Leon and Cariñena. Some may be rather "peasanty" for modern tastes, but all are of interest. The red and white Chacoli wines of the Spanish Basque country are petillant (semi-sparkling), very dry and traditional with the region's shellfish, or for aperitifs.

The Central Region. Much of the wine made here was, until recently, sold for blending or distilling. Today, some regional names are becoming known, thanks to modern methods of wine making and the influence of foreign shippers. Wines having a Denominación de Origen are: Almansa, La Mancha, Mentrida and Valdepenas. This is Don Quixote country and many of the wines, although modest, are pleasant drinks.

The Levante. Another region formerly mainly making bulk wines, as it produced deep-toned, buxom beverages, useful for "helping" more

WINES OF SPAIN

fragile wines elsewhere. Names to bear in mind today are: Valencia, Utiel-Requena, Alicante, Yecla, Jumilla.

The Balearic Islands and the Canaries. Wine is made in fair quantities on Mallorca, both red and white and that produced on the Benisalem estate is well reputed. But these holiday islands cater for holiday drinkers and only modest quality seems to have been achieved. Although Canary wine enjoyed a high reputation in the past and was referred to by Shakespeare (it then seems to have been mostly sweet), today the wines there are made for local everyday requirements.

Sparkling Wines

Vast amounts of sparkling wine are made, the main production coming from the Penedés region in the northeast. The so-called *cava* wines are made by the Champagne method: when one sees the huge installations, it's hard to realise that it was as recently as 1872 that the family firm of Codorniu, established in the 16th century, went in for sparkling wines. Today, this enormous winery at San Sadurni de Noya is bigger than any Champagne establishment. There's a wine museum here and well-organised tours can be arranged, with multi-lingual guides. Freixenet is the other giant, but there are many other firms. Most produce a range, from the very dry *brut,* through *seco* and *semiseco* to the *semidulce* and *dulce,* also some luxury blends. At the Castle of Parelada, to the north, there's also a wine museum, but this region is best known for Perelada sparkling wines, made by the *cuve close* or sealed vat method; the wine must be kept quite apart from cava wines and the corks have a black oval on their bases, whereas cava corks have a star.

Relevant Words and some Label Terms

If you want ordinary everyday wine, ask for *Vino corriente.* A *copa* is a glass, a *copita* is the tulip-shaped glass used for sherry. *Tinto* is red, *blanco* is white, *rosado* is rosé, *clarete* means a light-bodied red wine. *Reserva* implies a wine of some quality and maturity. *Seco* is dry, *dulce* is sweet, *brut* is very dry, *abocado* is medium-sweet. *Vino de mesa* and *vino de pasta* are both terms meaning table wine—and don't forget that, in the sherry region, a sherry may also be a *vino de pasta. Espumosa* is sparkling wine and one labelled *cava* means it will have been made according to the Champagne method. In fact it's illegal to refer to such wines as *Champana,* but Spanish waiters continue to do so!

Rancio doesn't mean rancid, but is a term used to describe the taste of a white wine that has been matured long-term in a cask, thereby being exposed to some air, which gives it a somewhat different flavor from the very fresh, light white wines made everywhere these days. A *porrón* is the curious flask with a long projecting spout, from which the wine can be poured directly into the mouth without the flask touching the lips—very hygienic when several are sharing the wine. Sometimes the experienced show off by sending the wine down their noses or pouring from the porrón held high above their heads.

The words *cosecha* and *vendimia* both mean vintage, and now that Spain has joined the E.E.C. use of these terms must comply with E.E.C. regulations. In former years wines labeled vintage did not necessarily come solely from one year—in some of the classic wines of Spain the casks were topped up or "refreshed" with other wine. Regulations were tightened in 1976, and now labeling is subject to the same controls as the rest of Europe.

A *bodega* really has two meanings: it's a term used to signify a wine shop, but is also applied to a winery, and therefore the word is often used in conjunction with the name of a particular firm.

Drinking Traditions

As you probably know, the mid-day and evening meals tend to be taken later in Spain than in other countries. This means that people can take their siesta during the hottest time of the day and then can enjoy a long evening.

You can usually get wine by the glass anywhere and in the sherry region you'll see sherry served throughout a meal, often in half bottles.

Traditionally, any aperitif will be accompanied by something to nibble, even if merely biscuits, olives and nuts. This is all part of the Mediterranean concept of not drinking without eating and these refreshments, known as *tapas*, can be quite elaborate, sometimes even sufficient for a mini-meal. *Sangria* is a refreshing mixture of wine and fruit juice, often red wine with citrus, but it can be based on white wine. It comes in a large jug, useful for sharing between several people.

A great deal of Spanish brandy is made, sweeter, heavier, and darker than Cognac. There is also a wide range of liqueurs—some of the world famous ones are made under license in Spain—and in most wine regions there are some sweet wines, suitable for drinking after meals.

In small bars and country restaurants, wine may often be served in large jugs, which are used to draw it straight from the casks. Here, you may be provided with tumblers rather than glasses with stems.

Visiting Wineries

In the sherry region of Andalusia, in parts of the Rioja area and in the Penedés, including the installations where sparkling wines are made, there are various good facilities for visiting wineries, plus English-speaking guides. The larger firms like to show interested travelers around, although sometimes they may seem to spend more time displaying modern vats, bottling and despatch departments rather than anything more obviously picturesque. Still, be polite and don't try to hurry a tour!

Elsewhere, and in smaller installations, you may find it harder to fix a visit, especially if you do not speak any Spanish. However, your hotel or the local tourist office may be able to arrange something.

Remember that at vintage time (September and October) installations tend to be hard at work and cannot receive visitors easily. During vintage festivities bodegas may also be shut, so ask before you try to

WINES OF SPAIN

get in. Also, and this applies for most of the year, wineries usually shut from about 1 P.M. for three hours.

Many of the larger wine firms have collections of exhibits to do with wine, often dignified as "Museums" and, of course, many general museums have sections devoted to local traditions, including wine making.

Wear walking shoes, for many installations are extensive, and take a jacket because cellars can be cool; those making sparkling wines are definitely cold. If a member of a firm shows you round, there is no need to do more than express thanks at the end of a tour, but an official guide may expect a tip—this is usually made obvious.

Further Information

The following are sources of information for anyone seriously interested in Spanish wines: I.N.F.E., Pasco de la Castellana, 14, Madrid - 1, Spain; Wines of Spain, Commercial Office of Spain, 405 Lexington Ave., New York, 10017, N.Y., U.S.A.; Vinos de Espana, Commercial Office of Spain, 55 Bloor St. W., Suite 1204, Toronto, Ontario M4W 1A5, Canada; Spanish Promotion Centre, 22 Manchester Square, London W1M 5AP, England.

Also recommended are Jan Read's books, *The Simon and Schuster Pocket Guide to Spanish Wines* (U.S.); *The Century Companion to the Wines of Spain and Portugal* (U.K.); and the detailed and scholarly *Wines of Spain* (Faber and Faber).

EATING IN SPAIN

Gazpacho and Garlic, Shellfish and Squid

Eating in Spain can be a delightful adventure or a sad disappointment. The traveler who has the good sense to hunt out local specialties and to choose carefully the restaurants where he eats can enjoy his trip to Spain for the food alone. But many hotels, particularly in the popular coastal areas, put on their version of an Anglo-Saxon meal, which is usually disastrous.

Spanish cuisine is neither so dainty nor so varied as the French or, perhaps, the Italian, but it has virtues of its own. It is substantial and plentifully served and still has its light and delicate dishes for hot weather. One virtue for the traveler is that restaurant prices are still very reasonable, though for how much longer remains to be seen.

The Spanish, as a nation, eat out a lot, hence the huge number of restaurants, many of them colorful and full of local atmosphere. Service, for the most part, is courteous and highly professional but don't expect it to be swift; that is not the Spanish way.

Spaniards do not like their food very hot. They say it has no taste that way. Those who like their food piping hot should insist with the waiter that it be served *muy caliente*. Nor is Spanish food highly seasoned, as many visitors expect it to be. In fact, cooking with chilli is almost unknown in Spain, and pepper pots are not commonly placed on tables. Olive oil is the basis of all cooking, and when well used you

EATING IN SPAIN

will hardly notice it. The same cannot be said, however, for the liberal use of garlic which dominates many Spanish dishes. If you really don't like garlic, avoid any dishes that are served *al ajillo*.

Meat is generally good though not outstanding. Pork *(cerdo)* and veal *(ternera)* predominate along with the ubiquitous *biftec,* generally a thin piece of beef rather than the steak you might expect. In fact, ordering steak is not usually the wisest choice. Roasts tend to be good in Castile and game, particularly pheasant *(faisán),* partridge *(perdiz),* and quail *(cordonices)* are quite common when in season.

Vegetables and salads are plentiful. It is customary to order vegetables as a first course, usually lightly fried *(salteados)* and mixed with oil, tomato or diced ham making a very tasty starter. Examples are *judías verdes con tomate* (green beans in tomato sauce), *champiñones al ajillo* (mushrooms sautéed in garlic), and *alcachofas con jamon* (artichoke hearts and ham). Cold vegetable starters include *espárragos con mahonesa,* canned asparagus tips which in Spain are traditionally eaten with mayonnaise rather than butter, endives and palm hearts. Spaniards usually order a mixed salad to accompany their main course and this is served on a communal dish into which everyone dips at will. The salad is rarely served with dressing already on it; instead you mix your own dressing with the oil and vinegar on the table.

Where Spain scores best on the gastronomic front is in the sheer variety and abundance of fresh fish and seafood *(mariscos)* on offer in almost every region of the country. The rapid and efficient transportation of freshly caught fish to all but the farthest flung reaches of the nation is one of the country's better organized features.

Merluza (hake) is found all over Spain, and when served well can be quite tasty though it is not the most interesting of fish. *Rape* (angler or monkfish) is another popular whitefish and with its slightly chewy texture makes good fish kebabs. Other commonly found fish are swordfish *(pez espada)* with its delicate taste and close texture rather like meat, and sole *(lenguado)* which is especially delicious served in an orange sauce. Tuna fish *(bonito* or *atún)* is served fresh in the north, cut into steaks and cooked in a rich tomato and onion sauce. It is even more plentiful on the Atlantic coast between Gibraltar and Cádiz. Fresh trout and salmon can also be had in season though be careful not to confuse *salmón* (salmon) with *salmonete* (mullet). *Trucha a la navarra* is a popular way of serving trout, when it is fried and stuffed with a salt cured ham similar to bacon. In San Sebastián, Bilbao, Málaga and other fishing ports, fresh sardines, grilled or fried, are popular. A dish likely to be strange to Anglo-Saxon visitors is squid, or cuttlefish, and it is well worth sampling. Known as *calamares,* or if small, *pulpitos* or *chipirones,* it is at its best in the Basque country and Catalonia. It is served either in its own ink, in a dark sauce, or cut up and deep fried in batter rings *(calamares fritos)* and in this case should be served piping hot and with lemon wedges. Another popular shellfish dish is *almejas a la marinera,* small clams steamed in their shells and served in a delicious sauce of garlic, olive oil and finely chopped parsley. Lobster *(langosta),* crayfish *(langostinas)* and shrimp *(gambas)* are plentiful and very good. *Sopa de pescado* is a fish soup not inferior to French *bouillabaisse,* though less complicated. Traditionally the staple food of fishermen, it is made with shrimps, clams and chunks of *merluza* and other dainties, and is to be recommended in most restaurants. *Zarzuela de mariscos* is another Spanish delicacy, if this is the right word for such a robust dish. Here a great variety of shellfish and white fish are first fried, then cooked in a sauce made up of onions, garlic, tomatoes, wine and laurel. It is served in many of the better restaurants.

One of the basic elements of Spanish diet is pulses—dried beans, lentils and chick peas. They are cooked in all sorts of ways and the dishes have different names in each part of the country. The Basques like white or red beans stewed with *chorizo*—a peppery red sausage—and blood sausage. Farther west, Asturias is famous for *fabada,* a sort of simplified cassoulet of white beans with salt pork and sausage. Each region has its bean dish. Madrid's specialty is *cocido,* made with big yellow chick peas. Boiled beef, boiled chicken, boiled bacon and other choice bits are served with a great dish of peas, preceded by a broth made with the water they have been cooked in. It is a meal all by itself. *Garbanzos* are chick peas served in an earthenware casserole with olive oil, tomatoes and chorizo. These pulse dishes tend to be filling and are best ordered only when you feel like something warm and very satisfying.

Spanish desserts *(postres)* are something of a let-down. The patisserie is a far cry from what Central Europe has to offer. The Moorish-inspired dry cakes, like *polvorones* (*polvo* means "dust" to give you an idea), *manoletes, yemas* or *roscas* are far too sweet for most Anglo-American palates. More often than not you will be forced to fall back on the ubiquitous *flan* (creme caramel). There is no need to despair however: Valencia oranges, melons, strawberries, Almería grapes, Alicante dates and wonderful peaches from Aragón can usually make up for this gap in Spanish gastronomy. But don't be tempted to choose fruit dishes served *en almibar* as this is the Spanish way of saying "canned."

Finally we come to cheese. The best known one is *manchego,* from La Mancha. It comes in various shapes, sizes and tastes but the best should be slightly moist and with a taste that stops just short of being sharp. Roquefort is also becoming popular, but by far and away the best blue cheese is a delicacy usually found in the north, where it is made in the Picos de Europa mountains. This is the famous *queso cabrales* made from a blend of sheep, goat and cows' milk and left to mature wrapped in a large leaf. It is also on sale in Madrid and Barcelona and if you have an opportunity to try it, is a real treat.

Regional Specialties

Most of the dishes mentioned above can be found throughout Spain, but in addition, each region has numerous local specialties. The parador hotels are good places to sample these, as they have a special brief to concentrate on their regional cooking. Here are just a few of the things to look out for.

Galicia. Galicia in the far northwest of Spain offers an outstanding variety of fish and shellfish caught fresh from its shores. Especially typical are *centollas,* a large crab stuffed with its own minced meat. *Empanadas* are a kind of pie, half way between a pizza and a Cornish pasty and may be filled with either meat or fish mixtures. *Caldo gallego* is a typical Galician broth and *lacón con grelos* a regional meat dish consisting of ham and turnip tops and generally much better than it sounds. Make sure you sample some of the rich Ribeiro wines traditionally drunk out of white china bowls rather than glasses, and a *queimada* or two, a glass of the local *aguadiente* set alight (its name means "burning").

Asturias and Cantabria. The verdant provinces of Oviedo and Santander are famous throughout Spain for their dairy cattle and milk products. Here is your chance to sample the superb *cabrales* cheese, or maybe a creamy *cuajada,* a thick set yogurt flavored with honey. Recommended in Santander is the dessert of "fried milk," *leche frita,* a delicious caramelized custard. Asturias is known for its bean stew, *fabada asturiana,* and for its cider *(sidra).* Besides being the only region in Spain where cider is produced and drunk, the Asturians have an amazing manner of pouring their local drink. Holding the pitcher above one shoulder, they pour it over the other shoulder into a glass held almost at ground level, all of which is no doubt intended to improve the sparkle. Good in Santander are *percebes* (barnacles) and some tiny prawns said to be unique to this city. *Cocido montañés* is a bean, cabbage and pork stew.

Basque Country. The Basques have the reputation of being great eaters, and the food of the Basque country is among the best in Spain. It is one of the few regions where good beef can usually be found, though the traveler who insists on steaks may be disappointed as veal is the Basques' own preference. They like hearty dishes and usually eat several at a meal. One of their specialties that has spread all through Spain is salt codfish cooked with fresh tomatoes—*bacalao a la Vizcaina*—and another is the same fish cooked slowly *(pil-pil)* in olive oil. *Merluza a la vasca* too is best served on its home ground. This consists of baked hake served in a casserole in a sauce of clams and shrimps, and garnished with hard boiled egg, asparagus shoots and peas. *Xangurro* a crab shell stuffed with its own meat and baked with rum and coñac is sometimes a little over-rated but is delicious when well done.

In winter their great luxury is *anguilas,* baby eels, cooked whole and served in sizzling hot olive oil with garlic and pieces of red-hot peppers. It takes nerve to try them the first time and it remains an acquired taste.

Following the vogue for *nouvelle cuisine* in France, *Basque nouvelle cuisine* has taken off in a big way and can be sampled not only in the Basque region but in many top restaurants in other parts of Spain, in particular in Barcelona's *Ama Lur.*

Aragón. Aragonese cooking tends to be reliable and basic and notable mainly for the quality of its fruit and vegetables.

Catalonia. Catalan cooking is notable for its liberal use of garlic, and tomatoes and peppers are also used lavishly. Spaniards, or rather

Catalans, say that many of the dishes served in France *à la Provençal* are Catalan dishes introduced by the Spanish-born Empress Eugénie and baptized with French names to avoid offending national susceptibility. For real garlic lovers, they have a relish made principally of garlic, on the style of the French *aioli*, but it is a little powerful for many foreigners. *Pan tomate* is something you will see in many typical restaurants. This is slices of bread spread with olive oil and puréed tomatoes and eaten as an accompaniment to many dishes, especially seafood.

Pasta dishes tend to be more popular in Catalonia than elsewhere in Spain, and cannelloni and maccaroni appear on many menus as starters. Snails too, are typical of this region, though you won't find them much anywhere else in Spain.

One of Catalonia's boasts is that its meat is usually better than other parts of Spain, because, in the foothills of the Pyrenees, there is good grazing. A local meat specialty is *butifarra*, a Catalan sausage.

Valencia and Alicante. Paella is now so universally popular that it is often thought of as Spain's national dish, but originally it came from Valencia and many of the best paellas are still to be found there and in the neighboring province of Alicante. Paella is based on rice, flavored with saffron, and embellished with many tidbits of seafood: shrimps, calamares, clams, mussels and anything else that takes the chef's fancy. Small pieces of meat and chicken are also included and the top is decorated with strips of sweet red pimento, green peas and succulent crayfish. It should be served in the shallow iron pan in which it has been cooked. Paella is made to order and will take at least 20 minutes to prepare so it is not a dish for those in a hurry. Traditionally it is eaten at lunchtime and not in the evening.

Valencia is also the orange growing area of Spain and its large succulent fruits are at their best around March. Alicante and Jijona are famous for their *turrones*, a kind of nougat made with almonds and other nuts and flavored with honey. The palm groves of Alicante province are also well known for their dates.

Castile. Castile is associated above all with roast meats *(asados)*. Segovia is one of its prime culinary centers and all its restaurants serve the specialties *cochinillo* (suckling pig) and *cordero asado* (roast lamb). *Sopa castellana* is also much served and is a clear broth with chunks of ham, hard boiled eggs and a liberal scattering of vegetables. The dessert *ponche segoviano* will appeal to those with a sweet tooth.

Toledo is known for its game dishes. Further south the region of La Mancha has a peasant cuisine of its own. *Migas*, a mixture of croutons, ham and chorizo, and *pisto manchego*, a strong tasting casserole of vegetables based on green peppers and olive oil, may not appeal to every palate, but you should not miss sampling the famous cheese *queso manchego*, here on its home ground, nor the delicate *flores manchegas*, a petal-shaped cookie.

Extremadura. This region, together perhaps with La Mancha, is one of the few in Spain where you are better off sticking to meat rather

EATING IN SPAIN

than fish. Sausages, hams and *chorizos* (a highly spiced and fatty salami-like sausage) have long been the livelihood of the region.

Andalusia. Seafood here is excellent especially in and around Málaga. One thing that deserves special mention is *gazpacho andaluz* whose popularity throughout Spain has ranked it second only to *paella* as the national dish. *Gazpacho* is a chilled warm-weather soup. Made with olive oil, vinegar and strained tomatoes, its predominant taste is of garlic. Diced cucumber, green pepper, egg, tomatoes and croutons are served as garnishes.

Almería is famous for its grapes and Málaga for its sweet muscatel raisins which are used in the making of *Málaga Virgen*, a sweet muscatel wine. In Granada the *tortilla sacromonte* is typical, a potato omelet filled with diced ham and mixed vegetables. *Tortillas,* by the way, are omelets in Spain and not unleavened bread as in Mexico. *Tortilla española* is a thick, chunky potato omelet and *tortilla francesa,* a regular thin omelet. Loja is known for its *sopa sevillana,* a fish soup flavored with mayonnaise and containing *merluza,* clams and sometimes shrimp, and garnished with hard boiled egg. Trout is also common here due to the nearby trout farms.

Breakfast and Other Snacks

No matter how well you have prepared yourself for continental breakfasts, the meager Spanish breakfast will almost certainly be a disappointment. A few of the better hotels now make an effort to serve something like an English breakfast, otherwise you had better brace yourself to be confronted by a plate of stodgy buns, known as *croissants, ensaimadas, suizos* or *madalenas,* usually dry and tasteless. The accompanying orange juice is often a disgrace to a country which grows good oranges. There will be a choice of tea or coffee, and hot chocolate may also be on offer. Many Spaniards skip breakfast altogether, making do with a coffee till they stop work for a mid-morning snack.

Chocolate and Churros. Churros are a kind of fritter deep fried usually in rings. They are eaten sprinkled with sugar, and are very popular at fiesta time. Some cafes serve them for breakfast but they are best when eaten piping hot from a *churrería* or a roadside stall, though the latter can cause digestive upsets if the oil is not too fresh. Churros are traditionally eaten with cups or tall glasses of hot chocolate.

Tea and Coffee. Tea is usually made with tea bags and served weak and on its own in the American style. If you want it with milk or lemon, ask for *un té con leche* or *un té con limón.* Coffee is served either black and very strong in a small cup *(café solo)* or with milk *(café con leche)* in a larger cup cappuccino style. If you want your coffee black but longer and weaker, ask for *un café americano.*

Ice Cream and Iced Drinks. Spanish ice cream is varied and delicious. A few particularly Spanish flavors are *almendra* (almond), *turrón* (nougat), *Málaga* (rum and raisin), *nata* (cream) and *mantecado* which is extra rich and creamy, similar to Cornish ice cream. Well worth trying in summer are the refreshing *granizado de limón* and *granizado de café*. Served only in ice cream parlors, these are lemon juice or cold coffee poured over crushed ice. *Blanco y negro* is cold black coffee with vanilla ice cream. *Horchata* is a delicious and exclusively Spanish drink. Served ice cold it looks but doesn't taste like milk. Instead it has a sweet and distinctive nutty taste for it is made from nuts. Look out for shops displaying the *Hay horchata* signs but beware the bottled variety.

Tapas and Raciones. Finally that most fascinating of all Spanish customs, tapas, those savory tidbits that you will see piled high on the counters of any bar or cafeteria. The variety of tapas on offer is immense: chunks of *tortilla, patatas bravas* (potato chunks in a spicy sauce), salamis, *chorizo,* cubes of marinated beef, squid, clams, mussels, shrimp, octopus, whitebait, fish roes, all served either plain or concocted into an elaborate salad. Ham is a delicacy—and often an expensive one. You can choose from either *jamón de York,* cooked ham, or the delicious and extremely rich *jamón serrano,* mountain ham, that has been laid out in the sun on the snow of the mountains, for the sun to cure it, while the snow keeps it from spoiling. It is a fine dark red in color, and when sliced thin, is translucent. Tapas are also served in larger portions called *raciones* and if you share three or four of these, they make a very adequate supper.

Worth observing is the "tapas and pastries ritual." Cafes and bars begin the day with their counters heaped with pastries. Around midday these are removed and replaced by the tapas for pre-lunch snackers. After lunch, at around 3 P.M., off go the tapas and back come the pastries which prove popular from 6–7 P.M. with afternoon shoppers. Finally, at about 8 P.M. out go the pastries for the last time and back come the tapas as the evening paseo and aperitif hour approaches. So, whichever of the two you wish to sample, make sure you get the timing right!

BULLFIGHTING FOR BEGINNERS

Art, Not Sport

Mention Spain to any non-Spaniard and one of the first things that springs to mind is the bullfight. However, although bullfighting may seem to be the national spectacle, you would be wrong to assume that every Spaniard regularly attends a bullfight or is even knowledgeable on the subject.

Far and away more popular is the national game of soccer (football to British readers) which the Spanish call *fútbol*. Spaniards pack the soccer stadiums of large cities during the season and are regularly to be found glued to their T.V. sets for a mid-week game. Soccer matches and bullfights both take place on Sunday afternoons but don't make the mistake of considering them rival sports, for the Spanish do not consider bullfighting to be a sport, rather it is an art form.

For the last 20 years or so the general popularity of bullfighting has waned considerably and so to a certain extent has the quality of the bullfights. Many of the regular Sunday afternoon fights are now little more than performances put on for the benefit of tourists. However, that is not to say that there are not still some excellent bullfights, most of which are held at times of major fiestas such as Valencia's fallas in March, Seville's Holy Week or April Fair, the Jerez de la Frontera Fair in May and the San Fermines bull runnings in Pamplona in July. In

Madrid around May 15 the festivities for San Isidro see some of the best bullfights in the country. At all of these times the fights are televised on nationwide T.V. and it is not unusual to see Spaniards all over the country crowding into bars or hotel lounges to watch the coverage. Good toreros are still held in great esteem and frequently make news headlines.

The ritual slaughter in the ring may have seen something of a fall-off in attendance but it is still big business. A top matador can earn up to $18,000 for one fight alone, spectators will pay up to $180 for a ticket for one of the top fights, and each year the Spanish government earns some $24 million in revenue from bullfights. In July 1985 a potential big boost was given to bullfighting by the introduction of "toro pools." It became possible to bet on the outcome of fights by guessing how many ears would be awarded. Half of the takings are returned in prize money, the other half, after deductions for expenses, are reinvested in bullfighting. As Spanish *fútbol* pools bring in some 2,000 million ptas. a year, the boost to the bullring is likely to be spectacular. Another proof that the popularity of the bullfight is far from dead came with Spain's negotiations to enter the Common Market, for no matter how hard the E.E.C. officials in Brussels insisted there should be an end to it, the Spanish were adamant: the bullfight would remain.

If you are dead set against bullfighting, there is no pressure to attend and you may be encouraged to know that there are anti-bullfight movements within Spain as well as outside the country; it is a debate which is given free rein these days. If you do decide to attend, you are quite frankly more likely to be bored during your first fight than you are to be revolted or deeply shocked, for appreciating a bullfight is a skill that can only be acquired with practice. The untrained eye will take in little at first and may quickly tire of the spectacle. So to help you understand something of what you will see, we offer the following pointers.

How to Watch a Bullfight

Anglo-Saxons, on their first introduction to bullfighting customarily voice an objection to it that indicates their lack of understanding of its basic nature. They consider that it is unfair. It is a contest between a man and a bull, in which the bull always dies. There is something wrong, they feel, in a sport in which the identity of the winner is fixed in advance.

So there would be, if bullfighting were a sport. But bullfighting is not a sport. Bullfighting is a spectacle. In a sense it is a play, with a plot. The plot calls for the bull to die. To object to that is as pointless as to object that the plot of *Julius Caesar* calls for Caesar to die. In another sense, it is a ballet. One of its essential features is the performance of stylized traditional movements, and a byproduct of their accurate performance is grace. In still another sense, it is an exhibition of physical dexterity, with the risk of injury or death accepted as the penalty for clumsiness, like the art of a trapeze performer. But in its essence, it is a demonstration of the mastery of a human over two living organisms —over the bull, for the point of the torero's art is to maneuver a thousand pounds of recalcitrant, malevolent armed muscle according to his will—and over himself, for perhaps the basic meaning of the bullfight is that it is an ordeal of the quality most prized by Spaniards, courage. The bullfighter must master his own fear before he can master the bull.

The brave man is not the one who does not feel fear; he is the man who feels fear and still faces the danger that frightens him. Bullfighters are invariably afraid when they enter the ring. Make no mistake about that. They are afraid, and they are right to be afraid. They know that their chance of dying in the ring is one in ten. They know that their chance of being crippled is about one in four. They know, usually, what the horn ripping through the flesh feels like; no bullfighters finish their careers completely unscathed.

The bull may always die (he can avoid that fate by refusing to fight, but this is rare), but he does not always lose. In that sense, bullfighting *is* a sport. But you will understand it better if you cease to regard it as a sport and look upon it instead as a spectacle—a spectacle to which death does not put an end, but is itself an intrinsic element.

The Plot

Bullfighting is a highly ritualized affair. All its details have been developed over a long period into a pattern that now never varies, each one ticketed with its own label in the extensive vocabulary of bullfighting. To begin with, the bullfight is not a fight—it is a *corrida*, a "running" of the bull. It is divided, like most plays, into three acts, the *tercios*—the act of the picadors, the act of the banderillas, and the act of death. There is also a curtain-raiser, the parade across the ring, in which all the participants in the coming spectacle take part, even to the men who will drag the dead bulls out of the arena.

The act of the picadors has scenes—the *doblando,* the first luring of the bull with the capes; the matador's first playing of the bull; the arrival of the mounted picadors to attack the bull with their lances; and the *quites*—which is the work of the matadors in luring the bull away from the picador. The fine points of these maneuvers will be explained in a moment.

The act of the banderillas also usually has three scenes, in the sense that three pairs of gaily decorated darts are ordinarily thrust into the bull's shoulders, but each of these scenes is the same.

The act of death, the *faena,* has two scenes—first, the playing of the bull with the small red flannel *muleta,* which replaces the billowing capes at this stage of the fight—and the killing with the sword—the moment of truth.

All of this you will see in every bullfight, good, bad or indifferent. How is a novice to know whether the manner in which it is performed is skillful or clumsy?

You may be surprised, at your first bullfight, to hear the crowd roar its approval for a maneuver that, to you, looks no different from those that preceded it, and were allowed to pass in silence. You may be baffled when seat cushions start flying into the ring, hurled by an angry crowd whose method of showing its ire is to attempt to trip up the matador and give the bull a chance at him. The fine points that arouse the admiration or the contempt of the crowd (and the crowd, at a Spanish bullfight, provides a spectacle second only to what is going on in the ring) cannot be expected to be obvious to a newcomer. You will undoubtedly know whether the performance you are watching is, in general, skillful or clumsy, for deft movements are graceful and awkward ones are not and it takes no expert to appreciate the difference between the single clean thrust of the sword that sends the bull down as though he had been struck by lightning and the blundering butchery marked by thrust after thrust, with the sword spinning into the air as it strikes the shoulder-blade of the bull instead of piercing through the opening that leads to the heart. But in order to know why a performance is good or bad, you will need some coaching.

What to Look For

The three elements by which the critics judge bullfighters (and the bullfight critic, in Spain, is a highly respected individual, whose verdicts can make or break a matador's career) are *parar, mandar* and *templar.* Parar is style, and consists in standing straight firmly planted, unyielding, bringing the bull past in a thundering rush with a gracefulness that gives no ground. Mandar is mastery of the bull, controlling his every move and spinning him about like a puppet. Templar is timing, and the acme of skill in this respect is to perform the maneuvers of the fight in slow motion. The more slowly the bull is moving as he passes the matador, the longer the time of dangerous propinquity lasts, and the more opportunity is granted to the animal to change tactics and go for the man instead of the cape.

Watch the matador's feet. He should not move them as the bull thunders past. If he really has control of the animal, he will make it avoid him; he will not have to move to avoid it. Watch how closely he works to the bull. Obviously his mastery of the beast must be more exact if he lets the horn graze his chest than if he pulls it by a foot away. Closeness can be faked. If the torero holds his arms with the cape far out from his body, if he leans well forward so that, without moving his feet, he can still bring the upper part of his body back when the bull reaches him, then he is not showing the same skill as the man who stands ramrod straight and maneuvers the bull without budging himself.

Some grandstand plays are really dangerous. Some aren't. Kneeling really is, because it reduces the mobility of the bullfighter. Passes in which the cape swings over the head of the torero are dangerous because it makes him lose sight of the bull at a critical moment. Passes in which the cape is held behind the bullfighter's body are also dangerous, obviously. Passes in which the bull, charging towards one side of the torero, is drawn across his body to pass on the other side are dangerous.

Psychology of the Bull

On the other hand, standing with one's back against the fence, which looks dangerous, often isn't. It depends on the bull. Most bulls have no desire to bang their heads against a hard wooden wall. It is often more dangerous, close to the fence, to allow the bull to pass between it and the bullfighter; bulls have a tendency to swerve outward from the fence. If you notice that the bull returns habitually to a certain spot in the arena after his various charges, it is more dangerous to fight him in that part of the ring than elsewhere; he has elected it, by some mysterious

BULLFIGHTING FOR BEGINNERS

instinct, as his home ground, and he is fiercer on it. It is more dangerous for the matador to taunt him into charging outward from this territory than into it. When he is returning to his base, he is intent upon getting back "home." He is paying no attention to the man who may happen to be standing on the edge of the path he is following. Bullfighters know that and sometimes take advantage of the bull's rush past to draw applause from spectators who haven't grasped the situation.

Paradoxically, the bull who looks most dangerous to you is the one who looks least dangerous to the torero—the one who comes charging into the ring full of fight and makes a vicious dash for the first bullfighter he sees. The type of bull that is out to kill is the type of bull the torero can handle. He has a one-track mind; and a bull with a one-track mind is predictable. You can tell what he will do. Therefore you can control him. Bullfighters like a fighting animal, one that is going to charge hard—and straight.

The Opening Scene

First of all you will need to identify the matadors. They will be the men walking in front of the opening procession into the arena, just behind the mounted escort. The senior will be on the right and he will kill the first and fourth bulls. The youngest will be in the center and he will kill the third and sixth bulls.

As each of the six bulls makes its entrance, its weight in kilos is posted at the edge of the ring.

When the bull first charges into the arena, one of the bullfighters will wave his cape at him and very probably, at the bull's rush, will dart behind one of the bulwarks that guard the openings into the corridor behind the barrier. Don't mark him down as a coward for that. It is all part of the ritual. The bull is not yet actually being played. He is being studied. Perhaps the first cape will be waved by the man closest to him, to find out if his near vision is good. Then a man on the other side of the ring will try, to test his vision at a distance. The matador is watching how he charges, and whether he has a tendency to hook to the left or the right. Upon his correct interpretation of the bull's reaction to these preliminary flaggings will depend his success in the rest of the fight.

After these opening evolutions, the matador comes out to demonstrate his skill with the cape. This is your first real chance to witness the art of the bullfighter. If, in reading bullfight stories, you have come across the term *verónica,* and wondered what it meant, it is probably what you are watching now. The verónica is the simplest and most basic of the various passes *(pases),* and it is almost always the one with which the matador begins. Its name, by the way, derives from the way St. Veronica is said to have held the cloth with which she wiped Christ's face. The torero holds the cape before him, more or less gathered into folds, his profile towards the bull, and as the animal charges, he spreads the cloth before the animal's snout, swings it by his body, and the bull follows it past. Ordinarily, as the bewildered bull turns, he swings him by again, then perhaps a third time, each time a little closer, as he becomes acquainted with the animal's reactions and acquires *mandar,* and perhaps finishes by gathering the cape in against his body in a half verónica as the bull passes. This usually stops the bull short, and the matador can turn his back disdainfully on the horns and walk away, a display of mastery over the bull that always brings a roar of *"Olé."*

The Picador

With the end of this scene, the picadors appear—the mounted bullfighters with lances. The object of this part of the fight is to launch an offensive against that tremendous hump of flesh on the top of the bull's neck, the tossing muscle. Until that has been tired, so that the bull will drop his head, he cannot be killed with the sword. The way to the animal's heart is opened only when the front feet are together and the head dropped.

The picador attacks the tossing muscle by meeting the bull's charge with his lance, which he digs into it. The role of the horse is to be tossed—not to be gored. He wears a mattress to protect him from goring and the management, which has to pay for the horses, sincerely hopes that it will succeed. But the bullfighters want the horse to be tossed. A bull whose tossing muscle has hoisted three heavy horses into the air is a bull beginning to be tired. There is also a second motive, to maintain the bull's combativity. He will not go on indefinitely charging into yielding cloth and empty air. He has to be allowed to hit something solid or he won't play.

There is perhaps one exception to the statement that the bullfighters want the horse to be tossed. The picador, though it is part of his job, isn't happy about it. When his horse is tossed, he goes down. The picador, unlike the horse, has no mattress. He does have a heavy piece of armor on the leg which is going to be on the side from which the bull will charge, and it is so heavy that when he goes down he can't easily get up unaided. He depends on his colleagues to draw the bull away.

Years ago, of course, the picador was even more vulnerable, because his horse had no protection at all against the bull. Everything depended on the picador's skill at holding off the bull with his lance. So many horses were gored, however, that the *peto* or mattress was prescribed. This last grew longer and longer until finally it began to scrape the ground. Picadors grew careless and sometimes jabbed away at a bull until he was half-dead from lance wounds alone. For this reason the size of the *peto* is now limited to about 60 pounds (instead of 90 or more), thus making the horse somewhat vulnerable and restoring a certain degree of skill to the picador's task. Horses are sometimes gored and this is often one of the nastier aspects of the fight.

Watch closely now, for here it is probable that you will have an opportunity to see some dexterous capework. The usual bullfight program calls for the killing of six bulls by three matadors. Although each matador has two bulls definitely assigned to him for the kill, at this stage of the fight all three will probably intervene. It is usual for the picadors to appear three times. The three matadors take turns in drawing the bull off, and in demonstrating their mastery of the animal. Thus this portion of the fight takes on the aspect of a competition among the three, and you may see exceptional brilliance displayed at this juncture.

Now you are likely to see some of the most intricate passes—though the chances are that at your first fight they will all look much alike. One pretty effect is to end a series of verónicas by holding the cloth of the

BULLFIGHTING FOR BEGINNERS

cape to the waist and twirling as the bull passes, so that it stands up like the skirt of a pirouetting dancer. This is called a *rebolera*. In the *chicuelina*, a rather dangerous pass, the matador gathers in the cloth just as the bull is passing, wrapping it around his own body. He hopes the bull's rush will carry him past, in spite of the sudden removal of his target. Usually it does. This pass is named for the bullfighter who first used it. So is the *gaenera*, which starts like a verónica, but in which the cape is thrown up over the head as the bull is passing. So is the *manoletina*, in which the cape or muleta is held behind the matador's back while the bull is invited to charge only an arm's length away.

The Banderillas

The planting of the banderillas—the pairs of decorated darts that are thrust into the bull's shoulders—comes next. This is a spectacular feat to the uninitiated, but it is in fact one of the least dangerous parts of the fight. Watch closely, however, if you see the matador himself preparing to perform this maneuver, instead of entrusting it to the banderilleros, which is the normal course. That means he is particularly expert with the darts, and you may see an extra twist added.

The Climax

The last stage of the fight, the *faena*, is the final playing of the bull and his killing. This is when the matador, at least if he feels he had a good bull, a responsive animal, bold and aggressive, will put on his best show. If, before advancing into the ring, he holds his hat aloft and turns slowly round, to salute the whole audience, it is your cue to miss nothing. It means that he is dedicating the bull to everyone, and that is done only when the torero believes he has an opportunity to give a particularly fine performance with all the extra, spectacular flourishes.

This is also the most dangerous part of the fight. For the large cape, the muleta is now substituted, a small piece of red cloth that offers a much less conspicuous target for the bull's attention than the matador's body. It is now that his skill will be exerted to its utmost and now that you will want to follow more closely every movement of the torero until at last the great black bulk of the bull goes crashing down onto the sand.

You may think that the quality of the bullfighting has suddenly decreased at the beginning of the faena, for there may not be much grace in the opening passes. That is because their object is to attain complete mastery over the bull. His will to fight is being broken, and it is done by violence rather than by grace. It is at this stage that you will see the faena's counterpart of the opening act's verónica, that is to say the most simple pass of this part of the fight, the *natural*. This consists in presenting the muleta, held out in one hand to the left side of the matador, and swinging it before the bull's muzzle as he charges. This is more dangerous when done with the right hand *(un natural con derechazo)*.

Once the bull has been shown again who is master, however, you may see some of the most daring and elegant passes of the whole corrida. Passes in which the matador stands erect holding the muleta with both hands, as though flagging the animal by, are called 'statues' —*estatuarios*. It is at this stage that you may see the *manoletina*, mentioned above, and some overhead passes *(pases por alto)*. The most dangerous pass you are likely to see now is the *arrucina*, in which the muleta is held behind the body. Also risky is the *pendulo*, in which the cloth is swung back and forth behind the matador's legs.

At the end of this demonstration, the time comes for the kill. First, it is necessary to square *(cuadrar)* the bull—that is, to maneuver him into a head-on position with the two front feet together. To judge this perfectly is an essential part of the matador's skill. For if he attempts to strike when the bull's feet are not perfectly together, or if its head is not lowered at just the right angle, or even if the bull moves his feet as the matador lunges forward with his sword, he will not make a clean kill. Instead the blade may strike bone and be sent flying high into the air leaving the bull writhing in agony and the matador needing to make another attempt. Such a misjudgement invariably elicits the wrath of the crowd who will start booing and jeering and possibly throwing cushions into the ring.

The Kill

With the bull fixed, the matador drives the sword in over the horns with his right hand, while his left, with the muleta, sweeps under his eyes and pulls his head down. It is a moment as dangerous for the man as for the bull; if the swing of the muleta fails to hold that head down, instead of sword into bull it will be horn into man. But if the matador has judged correctly, the bull crumples to the ground after a few moments' agony.

What the president of the fight, whose judgment is usually much influenced by the reaction of the crowd, thinks of the bullfighter's performance will be indicated now. If the matador did well, he is awarded an ear; exceptionally well, both ears; and for a really superlative performance, the ears and the tail. This is ordinarily as far as recognition goes, but there have been occasions on which a hoof or two has been added, and the all-time record is probably held by Carlos Arruza, who in Málaga was awarded the whole animal, at the end of a fight in which he had once been tossed. The dead bull may be dragged around the ring and cheered in tribute to his courage. This in no way reflects upon the performance of the matador—indeed, quite the contrary.

A few final points to bear in mind. A bullfighter is a *torero* (never, except in *Carmen,* a *toreador*) and only the star who kills the bull is a *matador (matar* meaning "to kill"). *Novilladas* are fights with young bulls and aspirant matadors, and for this reason, tickets are usually cheaper than for regular *corridas.* Should you come across a *rejoneador,* this is the revival of the old and spectacular style of bullfighting in which each phase of the contest is performed by the rejoneador mounted on a beautiful Arab horse which, needless to say, is kept out of contact with the bull's horns. It is closer to the Portuguese style of bullfighting than to the traditional Spanish style.

For information on purchasing tickets and tips on which seats to choose, see under *Bullfights* in *Facts at your Fingertips.*

ENGLISH–SPANISH VOCABULARY

Pronunciation. The important thing to remember with Spanish pronunciation is that the vowels are emphasized much more than the consonants.

Spanish pronunciation is always regular—once you have mastered the basic rules there are no exceptions to them. It is a very easy language to read and speak.

The Spanish alphabet has 27 letters; most are the same as the English ones, except there is no "k" and no "w." The Spanish alphabet has three letters that do not exist in English—"ch," "ll," and "ñ." When looking anything up in a Spanish sequence, "ch" comes at the end of the "c's," "ll" at the end of the "l's," and "ñ" at the end of the "n's."

Of the tricky sounds to pronounce the most difficult can be:

c   Can be hard as in "cat" or "cut"—casa (house); color (color) or soft and lisped, like "th" in "thanks." This happens before an "e" or an "i"—cielo (see-ay-lo), celoso (say-lo-soh).

d   Said as in English when it starts a word—data and delta; otherwise a hard "th" sound (like "this")—moda (mo-tha) meaning fashion or style; dado (dah-tho) meaning given.

j   A hard gutteral sound, harsher than the English "h" and made in the throat. There is no equivalent. Examples are—jamón (ha-mon) ham; jabón (ha-bón) soap; Jijona (Hee-hon-a) a town name; juro (hoo-row) I swear. If you have trouble with this sound, say it like an English "h" and you won't be far wrong.

ll   Almost the English "y." Llamar (ye-am-ar) to call; billete (beeyey-tay) ticket.

ñ   Nasal twang to an "n." Same kind of sound as in English "gnu" or the Italian "gnocchi."

z   The same as the lisped "c." "Z" is always lisped before *all* vowels. Zamora (Tha-mo-ra) a town name; zebra (thay-bra) zebra; zumo (thoo-mo) juice.

Basics

yes	si
no	no
please	por favor
thank you	gracias
thank you very much	muchas gracias
excuse me	perdóneme, perdon
sorry	lo siento
good morning	buenos días
good afternoon	buenas tardes
good night	buenas noches
goodbye	adiós
see you soon	hasta pronto
be seeing you	hasta luego
goodbye (literally "until tomorrow")	hasta mañana

VOCABULARY

Numbers

1	uno, una	16	dieciséis
2	dos	17	diecisiete
3	tres	18	dieciocho
4	cuatro	19	diecinueve
5	cinco	20	veinte
6	seís	21	veintiuno
7	siete	30	treinta
8	ocho	40	cuarenta
9	nueve	50	cincuenta
10	diez	60	sesenta
11	once	70	setenta
12	doce	80	ochenta
13	trece	90	noventa
14	catorce	100	ciento, cien
15	quince	1000	mil

Days of the Week

Monday	el lunes
Tuesday	el martes
Wednesday	el miércoles
Thursday	el jueves
Friday	el viernes
Saturday	el sábado
Sunday	el domingo

Months

January	enero	July	julio
February	febrero	August	agosto
March	marzo	September	setiembre
April	abril	October	octubre
May	mayo	November	noviembre
June	junio	December	diciembre

Useful Phrases

Do you speak English?	¿Habla Usted inglés?
What time is it?	¿Qué hora es?
Is this seat free?	¿Esta plaza está libre, por favor?
How much does it cost?	¿Cuanto vale?
Would you please direct me to. . . the bullring?	¿Por favor, para ir a. . . la plaza de toros?
Where is the station, museum?	¿Donde está la estacíon, el museo?
I am American, British.	Soy americano/americana, inglés/inglesa.
It's very kind of you.	Es Usted muy amable.
I don't understand.	No entiendo.
I don't know.	No se.

VOCABULARY

Please speak more slowly.	Hable más despacio, por favor.
Please sit down.	Siéntese, por favor.

Everyday Needs

cigar, cigarette	puro, cigarillo
matches	cerillas, fósforos
dictionary	diccionario
key	llave
razor blades	hojas de afeitar
shaving cream	crema de afeitar
soap	jabón
city plan	plano de la ciudad
road map	mapa de carreteras
country map	mapa del campo
newspaper	periódico
magazine	revista
telephone	teléfono
telegram	telegrama
envelopes	sobres
writing paper	papel de escribir
airmail writing paper	papel de avión
postcard	tarjeta postal
stamp	sello

Services and Stores

bakery	panadería
bookshop	librería
butcher's	carnicería
dry cleaner's	tintorería
grocery	tienda de comestibles
hairdresser, barber	peluquería
laundry	lavandería
laundromat	lavandería automática
shoemaker	zapatero (man), zapateria (shop)
stationery store	papelería
supermarket	supermercado

Emergencies

ill, sick	enfermo, enferma
I am ill.	Estoy enfermo.
My wife/husband/child is ill.	Mi esposa/marido/hijo (hija) está enfermo.
doctor	médico
nurse	enfermera
prescription	receta
pharmacist/chemist	farmacia
Please fetch/call a doctor.	Llame al médico, por favor.
accident	accidente
road accident	accidente de carretera
hospital	hospital

VOCABULARY

dentist   dentista
X-ray   rayos X, radiografía

Pharmacist's

pain-killer	calmante, analgésico
bandage	venda
sticking plaster	tiritas
scissors	tijeras
hot-water bottle	bolsa de agua caliente
sanitary towels	compresas higiénicas
tampons	tampones
ointment for stings	pomada para picaduras
coughdrops	pastillas para la tos
laxative	laxante

Traveling

plane	avión
hovercraft	aero deslizador
hydrofoil	hidrofoil
train	tren
boat, small boat	barco, barca
ferry	ferry
taxi	taxi
car	coche
truck	camión
bus, long-distance bus	autobus, autocar
seat	asiento
reservation	reservación
smoking/non-smoking compartment	compartimieto de fumadores/ de non fumadores
rail station	estación de ferrocarril
subway station	estación de metro
bus station	estación de autobuses
airport	aeropuerto
harbor	puerto
town terminal	terminal
sleeper	coche cama
couchette	litera
porter	mozo
luggage	equipage
luggage trolley	carretilla, carro
single ticket	billete de ida
return ticket	billete de ida y vuelta
first class	primera clase
second class	segunda clase

When does the train leave?	¿A qué hora sale el tren?
What time does the train arrive at. . . ?	¿A qué hora llega el tren a. . . ?
When does the first/last train leave?	¿A qué hora sale el primero/ último tren?

VOCABULARY

Hotels

room	habitación
bed	cama
bathroom	cuarto de baño
bathtub	bañera
shower	ducha
toilet	aseo, servicio, retrete; lavabo (in a train)
toilet paper	papel higiénico
pillow	almohada
blanket	manta
sheet	sábana
chambermaid	camarera
breakfast	desayuno
lunch	comida (de mediodia)
dinner	cena

Do you have a single/double/twin-bedded room?	¿Tiene Usted una habitación individual/con cama de matrimonio/con dos camas?
I'd like a quiet room.	Quiero una habitación tranquila.
I'd like some pillows.	Quiero unas almohadas.
What time is breakfast?	¿A qué hora sirven el desayuno?
Come in!	¡Pase!
Are there any messages for me?	¿Hay recados para mi?
Would you please call me a taxi?	¿Me llama un taxi, por favor?
Please take our bags to our room.	Nos lleva las maletas a la habitación, por favor.

Restaurants

menu	lista (de platos), carta, menú
fixed-price menu	menú del dia, menú turístico
wine list	la lista de vinos
waiter	camarero, mozo
bill/check	cuenta

ON THE MENU

Starters

aguacate con gambas	avocado and prawns
caldo	thick soup
champiñores al ajillo	mushrooms in garlic
consomé	clear soup
gazpacho	iced soup made with tomatoes, onions, peppers, cucumber and oil
huevos flamencos	eggs with spicy sausage and tomato

VOCABULARY

judías con tomate/jamón	green beans with tomato/ham
sopa	soup
sopa de ajo	garlic soup
sopa de garbanzos	chick-pea soup
sopa de lentejas	lentil soup
sopa de mariscos	shellfish soup
sopa sevillana	soup made with mayonnaise, shellfish, asparagus and peas

Omelets (Tortilla)

tortilla de champiñores	mushroom omelet
tortilla de gambas	prawn omelet
tortilla de mariscos	seafood omelet
tortilla de patatas, tortilla española	Spanish potato omelet
tortilla francesa	plain omelet
tortilla sacromonte (in Granada)	omelet with ham, sausage and peas

Meats (Carne)

cerdo	pork	jamòn	ham
chorizo	seasoned sausage	lechon(a)	suckling pig
chuleta	chop, cutlet	salchichón	salami
cordero	lamb	ternera	veal
filete	beef steak		

Poultry (Aves) and Game (Caza)

codorníces	quail	pato	duck
conejo	rabbit	pato salvaje	wild duck
faisán	pheasant	pavo	turkey
jabali	wild boar	perdiz	partridge
oca, ganso	goose	pollo	chicken

Variety Meats, Offal

callos	tripe	hígado	liver
criadillas	literally, bull's testicles (shown on Spanish menus as "unmentionables")	lengua	tongue
		mollejas	sweetbreads
		riñón	kidney
		sesos	brains

Fish (Pescados)

ahumados	smoked fish (i.e. trout, eel, salmon)	besugo	sea bream
		lenguado	sole
		merluza	hake, white fish
anguila	ael		
angulas	elver (baby eel)	mero	grouper fish
		pez espada	sword fish
arán, bonito	tuna	rape	angler fish, monk fish
bacalao	cod		

VOCABULARY

| salmón | salmon | sardina | sardine |
| salmonete | red mullet | trucha | trout |

Shellfish and Seafood (Mariscos)

almeja	clam	ostra	oyster
calamares	squid	pulpo	octopus
gambas	prawns, shrimp	vieiras	scallop (in Galicia)
langosta	lobster		
langostino	crayfish	zarzuela de mariscos	shellfish casserole
mejillones	mussels		

Vegetables (Verduras)

aceituna	olive	catabuna	raisins and pine kernels
aguacate	avocado		
ajo	garlic		
alcachofa	artichoke	guisante	pea
apio	celery	haba	broad bean
berenjena	egg plant	judía verde	green bean
calabaza	pumpkin		
cebolla	onion	lechuga	lettuce
champiñon	mushroom	lenteja	lentil
col	cabbage	pepino	cucumber
coliflor	cauliflower	pepinos	zucchine
endiva, escarola	endive, chicory	pimiento	green pepper
		potata	potato
ensalada	salad	puerro	leak
ensaladilla rusa	potato salad	seta	chanterelle mushroom
espárragus	asparagus	tomate	tomato
espinacas	spinach	topinambur, pataca	Jerusalem artichoke
espinacas a la	spinach with garlic,	zanahoria	carrot

Fruit (Frutas)

albaricogue	apricot	limón	lemon
ananás	pineapple	manzana	apple
cereza	cherry	melocotón	peach
ciruela	plum	melón	melon
fresa	strawberry	naranja	orange
fresone	large strawberry	pera	pear
		plátano	banana
grosella negra	blackcurrant	sandia	water melon
		zarzamora	blackberry

Desserts (Postres)

| cuajada | thick yogurt with honey | flan | caramel custard |
| ensalada de frutas, macedonia | fruit salad | fresas con nata | strawberries and cream |

VOCABULARY

helado de vainilla, fresa, café, chocolate	vanilla, strawberry, coffee, chocolate ice cream	pera en almibar	canned pear
		piña en almibar	canned pineapple
melocotón en almibar	canned peach	tarta helada	ice-cream cake
pastel	cake	yogur	yogurt

Miscellaneous

a la brasa	barbecued	guisado	stewed
a la parrilla	grilled	mahonesa	mayonnaise
al horno	roast/baked	mostaza	mustard
arroz	rice	pan	bread
asado	roasted	pasta	pasta
carbonade	pot-roasted	pimienta	pepper
espaguettis	spaghetti	sal	salt
fideos	noodles	salsa de tomate	catsup, ketchup
frito	fried		

Drinks (Bebidas)

agua	water	horchata	cold summer drink made from ground nuts
agua con gas	carbonated mineral water	jerez	sherry
agua sin gas	still mineral water	limonada	lemon-flavored lemonade
blanco y negro	cold black coffee with vanilla ice cream	vermut	vermouth
		vino	wine
		vino añejo	vintage wine
		vino blanco	white wine
		vino dulce	sweet wine
cava, champán	champagne	vino espumoso	sparkling wine
		vino rosado	rosé wine
cuba libre	rum and coke	vino seco	dry wine
fino	very dry sherry	vino tinto	red wine
gaseosa	English lemonade	zumo de naranja	orange juice
granizado de limón (de café)	lemon (or coffee) on crushed ice		

INDEX

Airline offices, 51–52
Air Museum. See Museo del Aire
Airport transportation, 28
Air travel
  from Britain, 2
  from North America, 2
Alba de Tormes (excursions to), 43
Americas Museum. See Museo de América
Aranjuez (excursions to), 43, 44
Archeological Museum. See Museo Arqueológico Nacional
Argüellas (area), 19
Army Museum. See Museo del Ejército
Art & culture of Spain, 59–60
Atheneum, the, 25
Atocha Railroad Station, 15
Auto rentals, 51
Auto travel
  from Britain, 2
Avila (excursions to), 43

Banco Hipotecario, 17
Bars & cafes, 39–40
Botanical Gardens, 15, 47
Botín's (restaurant), 22
Bus travel
  elsewhere in Spain, 30
  from Britain, 2
  in Madrid, 28–29
Bullfighting in Spain, 101–108
Bullfights 6–7, 48

Cafe Comercial, 18
Cafe Gijón, 17
Cafes. See bars & cafes & traditional cafes
Cafeterias, 38
Calderón de la Barca (house of), 27
Calle Arenal, 26
Calle Bailen, 24
Calle Carlos Arniches, 25
Calle Cervantes, 25
Calle Cuchilleros, 22
Calle de Alcalá, 16, 18, 26
Calle de Atocha, 15
Calle de Bailén, 23
Calle de la Cruz, 26
Calle del Carmen, 18
Calle del Prado, 25
Calle de Preciados, 18
Calle Fuencarral, 18
Calle Goya, 16
Calle Mayor, 22, 23, 24, 27
Calle Mira el Rio Baja, 25
Calle Princesa, 19
Calle Príncipe, 26
Calle San Martin, 26–27
Calle Serrano, 16
Campillo del Mundo Nuevo, 25
Carrera de San Francisco, 24
Carrera de San Jéronimo, 25, 26
Casa de Cisneros, 23
Casa del Campo Park, 20, 47
Casa de Lope de Vega, 46
Casa Paco (restaurant), 22
Casón del Buen Retiro, 14, 45

Castellana, the, 16–17
Cathedral of La Almudena, 23
Cava de San Miguel, 22
Cebada market, 24
Centro Colón (office complex), 17
Cerralbo Museum. See Museo Cerralbo
Cervecería Alemana, 26
Chicote's bar, 18
Chicote's Bottle Museum, 17
Church of San José, 18
City Hall, 23
Climate of Madrid, 1
Climate of Spain, 55–56
Coach Museum. See Museo de Carruajes
Columbus (statue of), 16, 17
Convent of the Descalzas Reales, 26–27
Corte Inglés (department store), 18
Costs in Madrid, 3–4
Credit cards, 4–5
Crystal Palace, 15
Cuenca (excursions to), 43
Cuesta Claudio Moyano, 15
Cuevas de Luis Candelas, 22
Currency & exchange, 3
Customs regulations
  American, 7
  British, 7–8
  Canadian, 7
  Spanish
    arrival, 3
    departure, 7

Decorative Arts Museum. See Museo Nacional de Artes Decorativas
Discos, 41
Discovery of America (monument), 19
Don Quixote & Sancho Panza (statue of), 19
Drinking water, 6

Electricity, 5–6
El Escorial (monastery), 27
  excursions to, 43, 44
El Palacio de Los Quesos, 27
El Pardo (palace/museum), 20, 46
Embassies in Madrid, 51
Emergency telephone numbers, 51
English-Spanish vocabulary, 109–116
Ethnological Museum. See Museo Nacional de Etnología
Excursions from Madrid, 27, 43–44. See also alphabetical listings

Fast food, 39
Fiesta of San Isidro, 11
Fine Arts Academy. See Real Academia de Bellas Artes de San Fernando
Flamenco shows, 41–42
Flea Market. See The Rastro
Food & drink in Madrid, 60–61
Food & drink in Spain, 94–100

Galeriás Preciados (department store), 18
Gardens of the Discovery of America, 17

117

INDEX

Glorieta de Bilbao, 18
Goya Pantheon, 46
Gran Vía, 18–19

Health certificates, 2
Hermitage of San Antonio de la
  Florida, 20–21
History & background of Madrid, 9–11
History & background of Spain, 53–61
History, art, architecture & literature of
  Spain, 62–83
Holy Week, 11
Hospitals in Madrid, 51
Hotels in Madrid, 30–34
  costs (typical), 3–4
  deluxe, 31–32
  expensive, 32–33
  general information, 30–31
  inexpensive, 33–34
  moderate, 33
  super deluxe, 31
  tipping in, 5
Hours of business in Madrid, 6

Information sources, 1, 28, 51–52

La Granja (excursions to), 43
La Mallorquina (bakery), 26
Laundromats in Madrid, 51
Local time in Madrid, 3
Lope de Vega (houses of), 25, 27, 46.
  See also Casa de Lope de Vega
Lost property information, 51

Mail & postage, 5
Malasaña (area), 18
Maps
  classical Iberia, 63
  Hapsburg Europe, 72
  Madrid, 12–13
  medieval Spain, 68
  modern Spain, 120–121
  wine regions, 88
Mesón de Drácula, 22
Mesón de la Tortilla, 22
Mesones, the, 22–23
Metro transportation in Madrid, 28
  map, 29
Monasterio de la Encarnación, 46
Monasterio de las Descalzas Reales, 27, 46
Moncloa Palace, 20
Motels in Madrid, 34
Movies in Madrid, 47
Municipal Museum. *See* Museo
  Municipal
Museo Arqueológical Nacional, 16, 44
Museo Cerralbo, 20, 44
Museo de América, 20, 44
Museo de Carruajes, 23, 44
Museo de Cera, 17, 44
Museo de Ciencias Naturales, 44
Museo de Escultura al Aire Libre, 44
Museo del Aire, 44
Museo del Ejército, 14–15, 44
Museo del Ferrocarril, 44
Museo del Prado, 11, 14, 45
Museo Español de Arte
  Contemporáneo, 20, 44
Museo Lázaro Galdiano, 16, 45

Museo Municipal, 18, 45
Museo Nacional de Artes Decorativas, 14, 45
Museo Nacional de Etnología, 15, 45
Museo Naval, 14, 45
Museo Romántico, 18, 45
Museo Sorolla, 45
Museo Taurino, 45
Museum of Contemporary Spanish Art.
  See Museo Español de Arte
  Contemporaneo
Museum of the Americas. *See* Museo de
  América
Museums in Madrid, 11–13, 16, 17, 18,
  20, 26, 44–46. *See also* alphabetical
  listings & *under* museo
Music in Madrid, 47

National holidays, 2
National Library, 17
Natural Sciences Museum. *See* Museo
  de Ciencias Naturales
Navy Museum. *See* Museo Naval
Neptune Fountain, 16
Nightlife in Madrid, 41–42

Old Madrid (area), 21, 27
Open Air Sculpture Museum. *See*
  Museo de Escultura al Aire Libre
Opera House, 23–24

Palace of the Senate (bldg.), 27
Palacio de Buenavista, 17
Palacio de Communicaciones, 17
Palacio de El Pardo, 20, 46
Palacio del Congreso, 25
Palacio de Lira, 19, 46
Palacio Real, 23, 46
Parks & gardens, 13, 20–21, 24, 27, 47.
  See also alphabetical listings
Parliament Building. *See* Palacio del
  Congreso
Parque del Oeste, 20, 47
Parque del Retiro, 15, 47
Paseo del Prado, 25
Paseo de Recoletos, 17
Paseo de Rosales, 20
Plaza Atocha, 13
Plaza de Cibeles, 16, 17–18
Plaza de Colón, 17
Plaza de España, 19, 20, 27
Plaza de Gabriel Miró, 24
Plaza de la Independencia, 15–16
Plaza de la Marina Española, 27
Plaza de las Descalzas, 27
Plaza de la Villa, 23
Plaza del Callao, 18
Plaza del Cascorro, 24, 25
Plaza de Oriente, 23, 27
Plaza de Puerta Cerrada, 22
Plaza de Santa Ana, 25–26
Plaza de Santo Domingo, 18
Plaza Dos de Mayo, 18
Plaza General Vara del Rey, 25
Plaza Mayor, 21–22
Police station (for reporting lost
  passports, thefts, etc.), 51
Prado Museum. *See* Museo del Prado
Public facilities, 6
Puerta de Alcalá, 15–16

INDEX

Puerta de Hierro, 20
Puerta del Sol, 26, 27
Puerta de Moros, 24
Puerta de Toledo, 24

Railroad Museum. *See* Museo del Ferrocarril
Railroads. *See* train travel
Rastro, The, 24–25, 50
Real Academia de Bellas Artes de San Fernando, 45–46
Real Basilica de San Francisco El Grande, 24, 46
Real Fábrica de Tapices, 46–47
Restaurants in Madrid, 34–38. *See also* cafeterias, traditional cafes & fast food
  costs (typical), 4
  deluxe, 35
  environs of Madrid, 38
  expensive, 35–36
  general information, 34–35
  inexpensive, 38
  moderate, 36–38
  tipping in, 5
Retiro Park. *See* Parque del Retiro
Ribera de Curtidores, 24–25
Riofrío (excursions to), 43
Romantic Museum. *See* Museo Romántico
Ronda de Toledo, 25
Royal Academy of the Spanish language, 14
Royal Palace. *See* Palacio Real
Rutas Verdes de Madrid (excursions to), 43

Salamanca (excursions to), 43
Salamanca (Madrid neighborhood), 16–17
San Fernando Fine Arts Academy, 26
San Francisco el Grande (basilica). *See* Real Basilica de San Francisco el Grande
San Ginés (church), 26
Security precautions in Madrid, 1
Segovia (excursions to), 43
Shopping in Madrid, 49–51
  antiques, 51
  books, 51
  ceramics, 50–51
  department stores, 49
  fans, 51
  Granada wares, 50
  handicrafts, 50
  main shopping areas, 49
  secondhand books, 50
  shoes, 51
  special shopping areas, 50–51
  stamp collecting, 50
  Toledo wares, 50
Sports, 48–49
Subways. *See* Metro transportation

Tapestry factory. *See* Real Fábrica de Tapices
Tascas (taverns), 10–11
Taxis in Madrid, 29–30
  and tipping, 5
Teatro de la Zarzuela, 25, 47
Teatro Eslava, 26
Teatro Español, 25–26
Teatro Royal, 47
Telephone Building (La Telefonica), 18
Telephones in Madrid, 5, 28
Temperature chart for Madrid, 1
Temple of Debod, 20, 47
Theater Museum, 18
Theaters, 47, 48
Tipping in Madrid, 5
Toledo (excursions to), 43–44
Torre de España, 19
Torre de los Lujanes, 23
Torre de Madrid, 19
Torres de Jerez, 17
Tourist offices in Madrid, 28
Tours of Madrid, 42
Traditional cafes, 39
Train travel
  from Britain, 2
  to other destinations in Spain, 30
Transportation
  in Madrid, 28–30
  to Madrid, 2. *See also* specific types of transportation
Traveler's checks, 3

University City (area), 19

Valley of the Fallen, 27
  excursions to, 43, 44
Victory Arch, 19
Visas, 2
Vistillas Park, 24

Wax Museum. *See* Museo de Cera
Wines of Spain, 84–93

Youth hostels in Madrid, 34

Zarzuela Palace, 20
Zoo in Madrid, 20

BAY OF
PLYMOUTH
ATLANTIC OCEAN
N
OPORTO
LISBON
El Ferrol del Caudillo
La Coruña
Gijón
Oviedo
CANTABRIAN MTS
Lugo
León
Santiago de Compostela
Ponferrada
Palencia
Pontevedra
Orense
Valladolid
Vigo
Tordesillas
OPORTO
Zamora
SPAIN
Freeways
under const.
Main Roads
Railroads
Car Ferries
Airports
Land over 1,000 m
0 kms 80 160
0 miles 50 100
Salamanca
Ciudad Rodrigo
GUARDA
COIMBRA
PORTUGAL
Plasencia
TAGUS
Trujillo
Cáceres
SANTAREM
Merida
LISBON
Badajoz
FRANCE
PORTUGAL
SPAIN & THE BALEARICS
Majorca
ALGERIA
Seville
FARO
Huelva
Gulf of Cadiz
Cadiz
TANGIERS

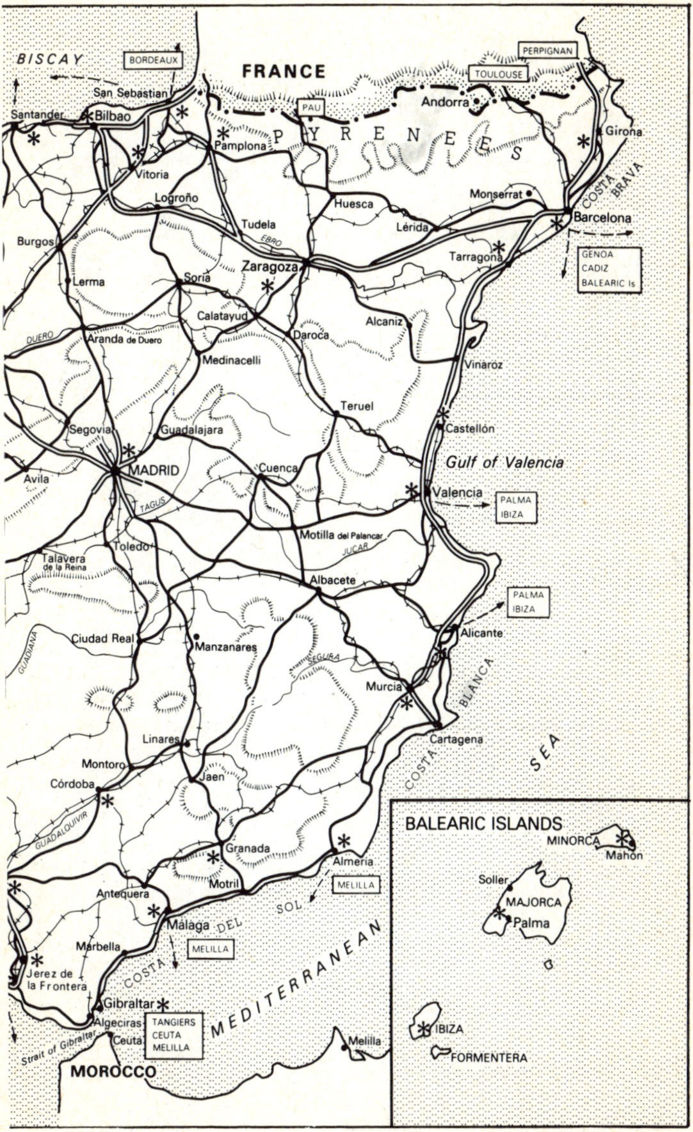
BISCAY
BORDEAUX
FRANCE
PERPIGNAN
TOULOUSE
San Sebastian
PAU
Andorra
Santander
Bilbao
Pamplona
PYRENEES
Girona
Vitoria
Logroño
Huesca
Monserrat
COSTA BRAVA
Tudela
Lérida
Barcelona
Burgos
EBRO
Tarragona
GENOA
CADIZ
BALEARIC Is
Zaragoza
Lerma
Soria
Calatayud
Alcaniz
DUERO
Aranda de Duero
Daroca
Vinaroz
Medinacelli
Teruel
Castellón
Segovia
Guadalajara
Gulf of Valencia
Avila
MADRID
Cuenca
Valencia
PALMA
IBIZA
TAGUS
Toledo
Motilla del Palancar
JUCAR
Talavera de la Reina
Albacete
PALMA
IBIZA
GUADIANA
Ciudad Real
Manzanares
Alicante
SEGURA
Murcia
COSTA BLANCA
Cartagena
Linares
SEA
Montoro
Jaen
COSTA
Córdoba
GUADALQUIVIR
BALEARIC ISLANDS
MINORCA
Mahon
Granada
Almeria
Antequera
Motril
MELILLA
Soller
MAJORCA
SOL
Palma
Málaga
DEL
Marbella
MELILLA
Jerez de la Frontera
COSTA
MEDITERRANEAN
Gibraltar
Algeciras
TANGIERS
CEUTA
MELILLA
Ceuta
IBIZA
Melilla
Strait of Gibraltar
FORMENTERA
MOROCCO

Speak a foreign language in seconds.

Now an amazing space age device makes it possible to speak a foreign language *without* having to learn a foreign language.

Speak French, German, or Spanish.
With the incredible Translator 8000—world's first pocket-size electronic translation machines—you're never at a loss for words in France, Germany, or Spain.

8,000-word brain.
Just punch in the foreign word or phrase, and English appears on the LED display. Or punch in English, and read the foreign equivalent instantly.

Only 4¾" x 2¾", it possesses a fluent 8,000-word vocabulary (4,000 English, 4,000 foreign). A memory key stores up to 16 words; a practice key randomly calls up words for study, self-testing, or game use. And it's also a full-function calculator.

150,000 sold in 18 months.
Manufactured for Langenscheidt by Sharp/Japan, the Translator 8000 comes with a 6-month warranty. It's a valuable aid for business and pleasure travelers, and students. It comes in a handsome leatherette case, and makes a super gift.

Order now with the information below.

To order, send $69.95 plus $3 p&h ($12 for overseas del.) for each unit. Indicate language choice: English/French, English/German, English/Spanish. N.Y. res. add sales tax. MasterCard, Visa, or American Express card users give brand, account number (all digits), expiration date, and signature. SEND TO: Fodor's, Dept. T-8000, 2 Park Ave., New York, NY 10016-5677, U.S.A.